READINESS FOR RELIGION

READINESS FOR RELIGION

A Basis for Developmental
Religious Education

RONALD GOLDMAN

A Crossroad Book
THE SEABURY PRESS
NEW YORK

Christian education of children

The Seabury Press
815 Second Avenue
New York, N.Y. 10017

First Seabury Paperback Edition, 1970
Eighth printing

Copyright © 1965 by Ronald Goldman

First Seabury Edition 1968; originally published 1965 by
Routledge & Kegan Paul, London

Library of Congress Catalog Card Number: 68-11589
ISBN: 0-8164-2060-2

Printed in the United States of America

In memory of
INGEBORG GURLAND

Contents

vii

Contents

Preface and Acknowledgments

M Y R E S E A R C H E S described in *Religious Thinking from Childhood to Adolescence* (Routledge and Kegan Paul, 1964) have aroused considerable interest among religious educators in Britain and in many other countries. I have been somewhat astonished and not a little embarrassed at the acclaim with which the work was greeted by teachers in all kinds of schools and representing all the denominations. What I had discovered by research had been felt intuitively for a long time by many teachers struggling to help children understand religious truths. It was a struggle, many reported, simply because little attention had been given to the development of children, with all their limitations of ability and experience, when the contents of religious syllabuses were drawn up. My first volume, therefore, was designed as a diagnostic guide to see what truths, in what form and to what level, children and young people could understand religion.

Because this was, by its very nature, a somewhat negative task, a natural question was raised at many teachers' conferences at which I was invited to speak. This question took many forms, such as: 'You tell us what the child cannot understand, and you emphasise the limitations of children. Must we give up religious education before the age of twelve or is there a positive

ix

Preface and Acknowledgments

alternative we can offer?' Or as another teacher wrote to me: 'You have clearly demonstrated the inadequacy of teaching scripture, but also you equally underline the religious needs of children. What kind of religious education is consistent with our children's total development?' It is easier to diagnose the problems of education than to suggest suitable remedies, but my researches and those of others have not merely diagnosed the current problems. There are positive pointers involved in the diagnoses which can help us to construct a programme of religious education upon a more realistic basis. It is the purpose of this volume to outline a programme of religious education more consistent with what we know of child development and more in accord with modern educational theory than the Bible-dominated programmes in current use. The Bible still remains the major source book of Christianity, but it must be used with greater restraint and with greater awareness than before if its usage is not to be a disservice to positive religious thought.

I am therefore indebted to teachers who have pressed me to develop the positive aspects of current research, and especially to Prof. W. R. Niblett, who, after a lecture I gave at the University of London, suggested that I write such a book. I am grateful also to Mr. Harold Loukes, for encouraging me to use the title *Readiness for Religion* as the title of this book. It is an appropriate description of what the book is about, since it deals with the kind of religion and religious teaching children and young people appear to be ready for at various stages of their development.

RONALD GOLDMAN

The Department of Education,
The University, Reading.

Religious truth is normal experience understood at full depth; what makes truth religious is not that it relates to some abnormal field of thought and feeling but that it goes to the roots of the experience which it interprets.

M. V. C. JEFFREYS: *Glaucon.*

The name of this infinite and inexhaustible depth and ground of all being is God. That depth is what the word God means.

PAUL TILLICH: *The Shaking of the Foundations.*

Where is the life we have lost in living?
Where is the wisdom we have lost in knowledge?
Where is the knowledge we have lost in information?

T. S. ELIOT: *The Rock.*

READINESS FOR RELIGION

PART ONE

The Psychological Bases

of

Religious Education

I

Why This Book Was Written

MOST CHILDREN in state schools in England and Wales attend morning assembly and receive religious instruction as a requirement of the 1944 Education Act. The indications are that a new Education Act will be drawn up about 1970 or soon after that date, and the debate is already beginning in public and in private as to whether the religious clauses of the 1944 Act should be continued or abandoned.

The debate is not due entirely to pressures from humanist, agnostic or other groups who are opposed to the teaching of religion compulsorily and who wish for a completely secular system of education. Nor does it seem to be due to the continuing decline of membership of the churches of all denominations and the fact that, in outward observances at least, we are ceasing to be a Christian nation. These factors contribute to the discussion but do not appear to be the major causes. The major cause is simply the ineffectiveness of much current religious education. After twenty years of this kind of teaching the results achieved are depressingly meagre.

Various surveys have indicated that at the end of secondary schooling knowledge of the Bible and even of what Christians believe is appallingly poor. Ignorance of many of the Christian festivals, the parables of Jesus and the nature of the prophets, and an incredible vagueness about the chronological order of well-known events in the New and Old Testaments, all indicate that despite the Bible teaching received after ten years or more under the Agreed Syllabuses, little of it seems to have registered. Moreover, research into the attitudes of adolescents indicate a serious deterioration in their feelings about the churches and the teaching of religion in school after the age of thirteen. Compulsory assembly and religious teaching has not apparently led to any increase in Sunday school or church attendance, or an improvement in confirmation or membership figures; indeed, the situation is quite the opposite, since the drift from the churches appears to have increased in the last four years.

It may be that the results of religious education cannot be calculated at all and that there are positive results of the 1944 Education Act which benefit individuals and society in an intangible way. It is difficult, if not impossible, to assess whether maturer relationships, greater moral determination, an increase in private devotions or a development of character have been the fruits of religious teaching. The increasing numbers of young offenders, larger numbers of illegitimate births to adolescent girls and reports of turbulent adolescent groups at seaside resorts are unreliable guides. The figures can be misleading and involve only a small proportion of the adolescent population. Yet those with high hopes of the 1944 Education Act at its inception are already thinking of these faults in terms of cause and effect and are wondering what use religious teaching is if it does not result in better morals.

The blame for this present state of affairs cannot be

laid at the door of the teaching profession, nor at any one particular door, for that matter. It is true that many teachers, not always committed Christians nor feeling themselves competent to teach religion, have taught it because they knew other colleagues would have to do their work if they contracted out. The result has been, to put it mildly, a considerable amount of poor, uninspired teaching simply because the teacher has been basically uninterested. By far the greatest number of teachers have shown a fine sense of commitment and have worked hard and conscientiously to make the subject a success. Many of these, however, confess to a lack of knowledge and training, and despite the increase of supplementary courses for religious specialists there is still a chronic shortage of teachers qualified and trained to take religious education in our secondary schools.

This secondary school shortage of specialist teachers has rendered many headteachers so desperate that they have eagerly accepted the offer of any teacher 'keen' to take the subject. Unfortunately, these are sometimes fundamentalists who teach the Bible with a complete disregard for informed biblical scholarship, encourage a crude literal belief in biblical narrative and make little or no impression on older, more intelligent, adolescents. They are rather like teachers of Biology teaching a pre-Darwinian syllabus completely unaware of post-Darwinian developments. Where this occurs in religious education a whole school population for many generations may lose the opportunity of knowing that people can be Christian without accepting beliefs which are an insult to their intelligence. Better training with more places for specialists would help this situation, but the

5

principal reasons for most of the ineffectiveness of religious teaching in schools lie in something much more basic. The root of it all lies in the assumption that religion can be taught as a body of knowledge to be absorbed by pupils, as other facts are learned. It is not regarded as a frame of reference, a cohesive principle, covering the whole of life, but as a series of facts or events mainly to be learned from the Bible. I would not dispute for one moment the centrality of the Bible for Christians and I regard it as the major document about which any informed Christian must be knowledgeable. But one may learn 'the Bible' and not be religious, since religion is a way of life to be lived, not a series of facts to be learned.

The results of this assumption can be seen in the many Agreed Syllabuses which may be justly described as Bible-centred. Syllabus writers have been concerned that pupils shall cover the Bible through their school career, starting with nursery school children right up to the sixth forms in grammar schools. The bulk of the material recommended for every age group is biblical and it is only rarely that non-biblical sources are recommended. Where they are it takes the form of Church history, Christian saints and heroes and similar 'religious' material.

It is true that in later syllabuses attempts have been made to relate them to children's experience and further efforts have been made to grade the material in what is thought to be ascending order of difficulty with increasing age. But the main weight of biblical teaching has remained as the solid content of syllabuses. For reasons outlined both in this book and examined in detail in my previous volume, most of our pupils find this content far too difficult. Parables for infant school children, the narrative of the Exodus for juniors, and teaching of the prophets to pupils in the early years in secondary schools are items of an intellectual diet which research demonstrates as unsuitable for children.

This unrealistic dominance of the Bible in teaching religion to the young is simply because when syllabuses were devised there was very little data available about children's religious development. In the last ten years a considerable amount of data has been added to our knowledge in terms of the thought, attitudes and behaviour of children. What it reveals is that the Bible is not a children's book, that the teaching of large areas of it may do more damage than good to a child's religious understanding and that too much biblical material is used too soon and too frequently. What it also confirms is that the content and methods used in religious education are out of step with educational practices in other subjects.

Implicit in the presentation of this kind of syllabus is the general idea that if only Bible stories or narrative are encountered often enough and attractively taught throughout a child's schooling, some meaning will rub off and stick, even though the details will be forgotten. In defiance of all sound educational practice it is assumed that understanding is not too important and that the sheer beauty and power of the narrative will leave some lasting impression. At this level religious education is reduced to conditioning, for by constant familiarity with certain stories we hope that suitable associations will be built up, much as Pavlov taught his dogs to salivate at the sound of a bell. Conditioning is not education; it is mere habit formation, and it is a poor foundation for a belief capable of growing to maturity.

I have deliberately over-stated the case, so that we may see it *in extremis*. It helps us at least to be aware of how far removed all this is from the real needs and capacities of children and adolescents living in the twentieth century. All the indications point to the fact that the answer lies in the needs of the children themselves. These criticisms are not criticisms of hard-working syllabus committees nor of individual authors who wrote much of the material. They were working in the dark, trying to provide intuitively what in more recent years we know to be an inappropriate diet for the young.

To return to the current situation, we can now see some of the deep-rooted reasons for so much ineffective religious teaching. It is difficult enough, over a long period of study, to understand the Bible for oneself. It is even more difficult to be able to translate what the Bible has to say to the limited experience of children of varying ages. I suggest that it is an impossible task to teach the Bible as such to children much before adolescence, and that we must look for another approach which offers a more realistic alternative to our present ills.

We have not very long in which to try this alternative, for unless religious education becomes more successful in our schools there is a strong possibility that a new education act will radically curtail, if not call for an abandonment of, the subject. I believe we have no more than ten years in which to demonstrate that an intelligent programme of Christian education, rooted in the children's experience, can lead to their more satisfactory religious development.

The situation does not call for the abolition of religious education, nor handing it over to the churches as is the practice in France, the United States and other countries. The current situation is one of unrealised opportunity where younger pupils are eager to understand, adolescents are hungry for spiritual guidance and teachers need help in their concern for the future of their pupils.

A number of books denouncing the present appalling situation have appeared and no doubt there will be more.[1] Their analysis of the problems are often cogent and penetrating but they offer no comprehensive or valid alternatives which teachers feel they can understand or accept. The time is ripe for a critical reappraisal of religious teaching but one which is positive rather than negative.

There has been some recent revision of syllabuses. These revisions unfortunately have, in the main, not radically altered the Bible-centred selection of materials for most schools. The sole claim to revision in some seem to be a redesigning of the cover while the content remains almost the same. The greatest help which our hard-pressed teachers need is not a mild revision but thorough-going reform of syllabuses in the light of evidence now widely accepted. The major finding supports a move from a Bible-centred content of religious education to a content which more closely approximates to the real world of children, using their experiences and their natural development rather than imposing an adult form of religious ideas and language upon them.

It is my belief that if syllabuses can be reformed in this way, religious education can have a new lease of life

[1] For references the reader should turn to pages 227-229.

9

and teachers can be rescued from the discontents and despair they often feel when faced with present syllabuses. If reform rather than revision can be the aim of most education authorities, their teachers will be profoundly grateful, and even those previously lukewarm will be attracted and encouraged to teach in ways which they clearly recognise try to meet the needs of their children.

This book is therefore written with some sense of urgency, not only outlining a programme of Christian education which research indicates should be the basis of reforms, but offering alongside it materials to be used with children which will implement such a programme. I would stress that this is not another scheme or gimmick which is going to result in the conversion of our nation to Christianity. Too much must not be expected from it, for there are deep social forces at work within our society, reflected in mass media and present in the life of many families, which create conflicts and tensions about religion. For this reason I have spent the first few chapters providing the reasons for my programme. Eager though the reader may be to see what I put forward as a new type of syllabus, my conclusions cannot be fairly understood without reference to both these early chapters and the researches which support these conclusions outlined in my earlier book.

2

The Children and Adolescents
We Teach

RELIGION is a life-long search, always incomplete. Even those who achieve a firm commitment to the Christian faith continue with many doubts, some beliefs being held more firmly than others. Always we are striving to understand more clearly, believe more strongly and behave more in accord with what we feel to be God's will. There are times when we wish to give up this search, and sometimes we do give it up and in periods of crisis we may start again with renewed interest. No one can give us religion, manufacture our belief or change our behaviour for us. Fundamentally we must grow as persons towards God, and although many things external to us can help or impede our development our religious growth is an individual and personal encounter with the divine.

If this is true of adults, it is also true of the young. In our concern to build a spiritual foundation for our children we have often been over-anxious to provide a ready-made religion, a complete system of beliefs and ideas, which we impose upon them. This is often done with great sincerity and from the best of motives, but in the long run it may impede a child's spiritual growth because passively acquired information is more quickly forgotten and ready-made religion is more easily jettisoned than where truth and belief have been the result of personal growth.

We find it difficult to accept an infant's religion as infantile and children's beliefs as immature when we have no such difficulties about children's mathematical or literary immaturity. In the past, until research enlightened us, we expected far too much of children and set them incredibly difficult tasks in arithmetic and reading at a very early age. We even punished them for misunderstanding what they were basically incapable of understanding. Perhaps the most striking achievement of child psychology has been the education of teachers in the intellectual, emotional and social development of their pupils, so that the content of what is taught and the methods by which children are taught are now more in accord with the real capacities and needs of children at the various stages of their development.

Until recently little was known about the ways in which children matured in religious development, so that it is not surprising that religious education has lagged behind the teaching of other subjects. In the last few years, however, a considerable amount of research has been made in this field, with some far-reaching implications for religious education.[2] We now know more about how children understand, and misunderstand, religious teaching, about the growth and deterioration of attitudes to religion and especially to the teaching of religion as a school subject. More also is known about children's limitations and their possibilities of spiritual growth. Rather than discuss this in general terms we shall look at some fairly typical pupils of varying ages, quoted from research material.

PORTRAIT OF A SIX-YEAR-OLD

Caroline is 6:2 years old with an estimated intelligence quotient of 105. She lives on a council housing estate and goes to an infant school which uses informal activity methods. The only subject not taught in this manner is religious education. Caroline's father is a building trade teacher in a local technical college and her mother does not go out to work, having a younger child to care for. Neither parents go to church, describing themselves as 'lapsed Church of England'. Nevertheless, they encourage Caroline to go to Sunday school. Her attendance is fairly regular in winter, but on fine days in spring and summer the Sunday family trip in the car has priority.

She is a gay little girl, often very thoughtful and greatly interested in everything around her. Her friendships are typically used to exploit other children, and she is in turn cheerfully willing to be exploited by her friends. She is on her first reader and is just mastering the skill of reading. She can write simple sentences with effort, and she enjoys drawing and painting. Dancing, in music-and-movement, is what she likes best in school.

Sunday school is enjoyed, especially the drawing of pictures, and hymn-singing when she knows the words. But she expresses dislike of having to read out in class and church services which go on for a long time—'I got so sore and tired.' She says that going to Sunday school helps her to do her day-school work, such as drawing. She feels church is a special place because it has special doors and coloured windows and people go there to sing.

Caroline prays every night before going to sleep when Mummy tucks her in. Prayers are addressed to Jesus, although the words 'Jesus' and 'God' are used interchangeably. Her prayers are largely egocentric and materialistic. Even when she prays for other people, such as 'my friends' she asks God to make them good friends. There are some prayers of thanks, mainly for food, toys or presents received. There is no problem of unanswered prayer for her since 'they all come true'. Sometimes she says, 'a boy who has been naughty or has not said "please" won't get anything'.

God is a man, wearing 'a long sort of white shawl'. He'd be a special sort of man, not like other men, and he'd have a kind face. Caroline feels God is everywhere and this is what is special about him because the world is physically an extension of himself. The picture she drew, depicted at the beginning of Part 1, vividly illustrates this very materialistic physical and pantheistic idea. God lives 'in a far-off place in the sky' despite the fact that he 'is the world' and only comes back rarely to the earth. He used to visit people a lot 'in olden times' but not much now 'because we are naughty'.

Caroline pictures God rather like a human magician. He has a powerful voice, 'like thunder', which frightens people. He is very unpredictable and personally engineers thunderstorms and other acts of nature. She believes firmly that God loves everyone, but naughty people are vengefully treated and it is evident that God's unpredictable behaviour in the world of nature extends to his relationships with children. 'God can be unfair if he wants, 'cause he can do anything' is how she expresses it. The Bible was 'dictated by God, and Jesus took it down on his typewriter' she states solemnly. It is a book to be thought of in magical and awesome terms and, because it is written by God, it is entirely and literally true.

Jesus is seen as a mixture of a simple, holy man who helped people and is also something of a magician. Caroline has a rather sentimental picture of him as an angelic boy 'born in that stable with angels and light and shepherds'. 'When he growed up he was good too,' but it is clear that Caroline thinks all grown-ups share this perfection, simply because they cease to be children. Evil is something spectacular, demonstrated by thieves and murderers, rather than a general human condition.

To sum up Caroline's religious development at this age we can say that emotionally she has positive attitudes to religion, she accepts happily and uncritically everything associated with God. It is very much a fairy-tale level of religion in which fairies, Father Christmas and other myths are put on an equal footing with God. She uses a large number of religious words, which she clearly does not understand. Many ideas are drastically misunderstood because her reasoning is far from logical, she finds difficulty in relating one idea to another, and anything of an abstract nature is beyond her. Concepts of God are crudely anthropomorphic and her ideas of prayer are magical. There is a refreshingly simple and naïve pantheism about her view of God.

PORTRAIT OF A NINE-YEAR-OLD

Peter is of average intelligence with an age of 9:10, living in a suburban area of small privately-owned semi-detached houses. The junior school he attends is a mixture of formal and informal methods of teaching, religious education being among the most formal. Father is a semi-skilled engineering worker. Mother does some cleaning at a nearby house·three mornings a week. Peter has two elder brothers with whom he goes regularly to a Free Church Sunday school, and he reads a short portion of scripture each day as a member of the I.B.R.A. The parents express interest but rarely go to church, only on occasions such as Christmas or aniversary events.

A very active boy, Peter wants to be a professional footballer and collects pictures of top football players as a hobby. He is good with his hands, but enjoys reading, especially adventure stories and books related to sport. He has two very close friends and the three of them are members of a boys' group at school, which occasionally terrorises the playground. His favourite subjects apart from games are nature study and scripture.

Peter is not as enthusiastic about Sunday school as he was last year, since some popular members of his school 'gang' do other, more interesting, things together on a Sunday afternoon. He expresses some boredom at 'the long talks' but is very interested in Scripture stories. He likes the singing, especially hymns with a chorus. The Church and its attached Sunday school appear to him to be a place to go to learn about Jesus. It helps with Scripture at day school, 'you have a better chance of answering teacher's questions' and it also 'helps you to keep out of danger'.

Peter prays practically every evening before going to sleep and God is usually addressed, although Jesus is sometimes. He prays that God shall 'be with me night and day and keep me safe from danger'. He prays for members of his family and for birds and animals, all 'to be kept safe'. He prays for 'poor people who need help and rich people, to give poor people money'. He feels most of his prayers are answered, simply because having prayed to be protected from danger, no mishap has occurred. His unanswered prayers he feels are the result of asking for too much or because he has 'done something wrong'.

God, to Peter, is a man, just as he is to Caroline, and he is conceived as having a beard and wearing a long striped jacket. Yet there is a difference in that God is thought of in a much more supernatural than superhuman way. Angels, golden thrones, souls of dead people and 'the glory' (Peter describes it as 'a beautiful golden glow') attend God. Limiting human elements are still evident, in that God still speaks with a human voice and operates in a physical manner in the scripture stories which Peter reads. He evinces a great deal of confusion about these scripture stories, being unable to transcend their concrete imagery and language, and as a result accepts them at a literal level, although plainly dissatisfied with his explanations. For example, if in a story God is present, as in the Burning Bush, he cannot reconcile God being in one place and everywhere at the same time. He solves these and other problems mainly by ignoring them and by beginning to separate 'the religious' from the rest of experience. One is a world in which anything can happen, where God behaves arbitrarily, but usually on behalf of his favourites. The other is a world of observable common sense, of natural law beginning to be discerned and where fairly predictable effects follow upon certain causes.

This dualistic view of life is further strengthened by how Peter regards the Bible. It is a story of long ago and far away and is not seen as very relevant to modern times. For all his frequency of Bible reading, Peter says little of it can happen these days 'because God has gone away. He don't speak to anyone down here now.' Perhaps this is why Peter feels it important to stick to the literal truth of the Bible. He does not distinguish between the Old and New Testaments, and the Bible was written by 'Siples of Jesus, Matthew, Mark and Luke'. Even though he has teachers who interpret the Bible to him non-literally, Peter feels it all must be really true. His reasons are simple and clear. 'It's all true because it's about God and Jesus. If the stories weren't true God would be a liar.'

Because of this strong literalism Peter sees no contradiction between differing Bible stories; all are equally valid and true. The love of God for all men is asserted and yet God may destroy whole groups of people because they are naughty. Peter sometimes feels God may be reluctant to take such extreme action but 'after all, he *is* God'.

Although Peter sees Jesus as a normal boy, engaging in a normal boy's mischevious pranks, the man Jesus he sees plainly as a master magician. He is fascinated by miracles, which 'explain' so much that happened long ago, but these are not related in any way to real life today.

In summarising Peter's religious development we can see many immaturities remaining although many immaturities which we recognised in Caroline have disappeared. For example, his ideas on prayer are still semimagical, but there are the beginnings of a wider sympathy and less egocentric praying. His attitudes to religion are positive and he is able to relate a number of ideas together, even if only at a concrete level. This lifts him beyond Caroline's unrelated and fantasised world, where trivialities are important, but it leads him to a literal and still physical understanding of the world of religion. The beginnings of a new understanding are evident, and he is preparing for the next step, when he tries to make sense of the mass of fact. Yet he is held back because he has no clear idea of what the Bible is and his intensive reading of it, far from helping him, seems to reinforce the crude literalisms in which he seeks an explanation.

PORTRAIT OF A FOURTEEN-YEAR-OLD

Olive is in her last year at a secondary modern school, is aged 14:2 and has an I.Q. of 108. Her father is a postman and the family live in a flat over the sub-post office below. Her mother helps her father run this. Olive hopes to stay on at school to continue a catering course, since she aspires to be a pastry cook. Her best subjects are those connected with domestic science. She has one very close girl friend in whom she confides everything and has been out with boys, but has no regular boy friend. Olive's major interests are cooking, clothes, 'pop' music and boys. When she began menstruation at 12½ years she was very worried and at times frightened. She knows quite a lot of sex information, but is very confused about how to behave.

Her parents are regular Church of England attenders and until she was eleven years old Olive went to the local Anglican Church Sunday school. When she found she wasn't to be moved up into the next group in Sunday school 'the Seniors' at the same time as she started secondary school, Olive continued for a few weeks and then left. 'I didn't want to be with children,' she said. While she is not hostile to religious knowledge, she expresses some boredom with it and thinks a lot of it irrelevant to 'real life', 'rather childish'. 'I'm tired of hearing those old stories so many times.'

In a recent test Olive knew why Christmas and Easter were observed, but did not know what Ascension Day or Whitsuntide were for. She could name two miracles of Jesus but no Old Testament prophet, and could not place seven prominent Old Testament events in correct chronological order. In placing New Testament events in the right order, Olive was more successful, but still misplaced one event out of five. In answering a question on 'What is a Christian?' it was clear that Olive felt any good person who believed in God, not necessarily connected with Jesus Christ, should be called a Christian.

It is evident that where the Bible is concerned, Olive had begun to develop negative attitudes, in her franker moments expressing a refusal to believe it to be true. She feels most of the stories are true about Jesus, but miracles, creation, many difficult passages and the 'queer language' make her regard the Bible as an irrelevant and useless book. She does not like teachers who make her read the Bible and 'tell me what it's supposed to mean. I like discussing and finding it out for myself.' She says, 'I would like real problems to be discussed' and it is clear that by real problems she means mainly the personal relationships and behaviour queries of a growing adolescent.

In her ideas of God, Olive still thinks in human

terms, but has begun to use and to grasp more abstract, and therefore more spiritual, ideas of God. She speaks of God as love and goodness, and as a spirit, although there is some confusion about 'the Holy Ghost'. Childish images still persist and the two worlds of the supernatural and the natural, beginning in Peter at nine years of age, have now crystallised into two separate and almost unrelated areas of experience. An example of this is to be seen in how Olive regards Jesus. Vestiges of him as a master-magician still remain in her mind. Unless 'what happened then can happen now' she cannot see the worth of the Bible. Since she feels miracles do not happen any more it is plain that the world of the Bible and the modern world have little in common in her view. The possible bridge across seems to be the ethical demands of Jesus.

Olive gave up regular bed-time prayers when she stopped going to Sunday school. She now prays occasionally, usually when worried or when some crisis occurs. Her prayers are very introspective and predominately they are prayers of confession and forgiveness.

It is plain that Olive's development intellectually has liberated her from much of her childish concrete thinking and she is capable of a more spiritual level of thought because she can deal with some abstractions. Yet in terms of her emotional life she is fast developing negative attitudes towards religion which interfere with any objective assessment of what Christianity is and what Christians believe. She appears to be well on the way to rejecting Christianity before she has fully comprehended what it means, largely due to a number of 'childish' associations with the content of religious teaching and the way in which religion is taught.

PORTRAIT OF AN EIGHTEEN-YEAR-OLD

Harry is 18:7 and is in the Upper Sixth of a boys' grammar school. He is hoping to gain admission in the following autumn to a university medical course. He has an I.Q. of 137. Both parents are teachers and he has an elder brother already at a university. He lives in a small detached house on a private housing estate within walking distance of his school. Harry is a communicant member of the main Methodist church in the town and attends the Young People's Guild. His parents are members and regular attenders in the same church.

Harry describes himself as 'an unorthodox Christian' because he cannot 'with my scientific approach to things' accept some of the Creed. He believes firmly in God, and in Christ as the Saviour, and in the role of the church in society, although he says 'I'm bored by a lot of churchiness, and some of our preachers seem a hundred years out of date'. Yet he enjoys much of his local church life, especially the guild, and sees the church not as a place, but a group of believers who support each other and face life together.

Looking back to his religious education in the state school system, Harry puts his views plainly. 'Up to the sixth form, where we could let rip and discuss things for ourselves, I think Religious Knowledge periods were a complete waste of time. We were given Bible stories, most of which we'd already had in junior school, and it was a bit of a farce, because we couldn't really question it. It was taught as history and, of course, most of us quickly began to reject it. It wasn't until the Lower Sixth that we learned there was an intelligent alternative to swallowing the Bible whole, as the whale is alleged to have swallowed Jonah.' At thirteen years he almost stopped going to church, and he felt at this time it was only the sympathy and example of his parents, especially his mother, who helped him through this period until he took the step of church membership. Harry expresses real anger that a non-literal alternative to Scripture was not given sooner and says many of his friends never recovered from what they called 'a betrayal'.

Concerning his present needs, Harry feels that he and his friends need to 'lay some foundations for modern life'. More specifically too he observes, 'Religion is essentially love, and yet few religious people want to talk to us about sex.' Subjects such as social justice, race relations and the problem of pain are the kind of things young people need to discuss, he says.

He still finds the Bible a confusing book, but reads it when he wants to consult some specific passage. He prays daily and finds family grace at mealtimes a strengthening habit to observe. Despite his obvious self-confidence and mature observations, he confesses to some anxiety about his medical course, not least the effect of it upon his faith. 'I hope I have enough belief to hold on to.'

COMMENT UPON THE PORTRAITS

I do not claim that the four pupils used as illustrations are completely typical of their age, but they are selected as representative of the stages most children appear to pass through in their religious development. Caroline at six is intellectually in a pre-religious stage where she has no real insight into a religious view of

life, where religious experience, language and thought
are merged so completely in her general experience that
their significance escapes her. Her understanding is indicated more by fantasy and feeling than by logic.
Peter, at nearly ten years of age, is much more logical,
but is in what I would term a sub-religious stage, where
a materialistic and physical approach is dominant,
rather akin to the earlier, cruder ideas seen in early
Judaism. Vengeance, inconsistent behaviour on the part
of God and spectacular intervention are all part of his
theological world view. Peter is gradually experiencing
the beginnings of dissatisfaction with these primitive
ideas. Olive at fourteen has found her intellectual concept of religion subject to many tensions, and like many
children not particularly gifted intellectually, has negative attitudes building up which inhibit her religious
belief. This is the personal religion stage, in which some
commitment for or against is imminent. Olive has
already moved over to the 'against' side, whereas Harry
at eighteen, after a period of uncertainty and some
antagonism, has worked through to a positive accep-
tance 'for' religion.

Caroline and Peter are real children, and Olive and
Harry are real adolescents, not obscure psychological
categories, and they are present in our schools in their
tens of thousands. How and when they pass from a pre-
religious, into a sub-religious and thence to a personal
religious phase and what are the implications for
religious education, will be explored in the remainder of
this book. In the next chapter I shall try to clarify what
limitations stem from these three phases before I turn
to the more positive recommendations towards which
research seems to point.

3
Developmental Limits in Religious Growth

W E D O N O T expect a week-old baby to walk, and a five-year-old to read the first leader in *The Times*, nor a twelve-year-old to master the philosophy of Kant. Exceptional geniuses there are who develop extraordinary skills very early, but for the vast majority of children we recognise that there are limitations to growth imposed by immaturities of various kinds. Failure to recognise the precise nature of these limitations has in the past, as we have noted, resulted not only in mental cruelty to children but also in a great deal of inefficient and misapplied educational effort. In such subjects as reading, arithmetic, writing, foreign languages, history, geography and science it is generally recognised that developmental limits exist and what we teach younger children has been modified to contend with their immaturities. In the teaching of a modern language, for example, a great deal of spoken French, using a conversational everyday vocabulary, now precedes the teaching of grammar, which is an essentially analytical and more complex activity. This thinking has further influenced the teaching of ancient languages and conversational Latin has begun to appear in some schools.

Developmental limits do not mean we should wait passively while maturation, the natural process of growth, occurs. The limitations of the young may be due to their rate of natural growth, but may also be caused by their sheer inexperience. If certain experiences are made available to a child earlier than he would normally encounter them these limits may be pushed further back to an earlier age. This in fact is the function of education. Teachers and parents try to enrich the life of the child so that he grows in understanding as quickly and as fruitfully as his maturation will allow. The major problem is to know what experiences and teaching to supply which are consistent with his development. Supply too little experience and push not at all, and development is slow; supply too much or inappropriate stimulation, and development may be arrested because the process is a forced and unnatural one. A realistic sense of this balance between waiting and stimulating is the most valuable knowledge any teacher can possess. It is no less important for the religious educator.

Religious growth is not something separate from the rest of a child's development. It is an interpretation of all his experiences, which he relates to what he believes to be the nature of the divine. In a sense, religious growth is dependent upon all other growth, since unless a child has a fairly wide range of experiences to draw upon he cannot begin to interpret and relate them to a theological world view. In other words, there is a time-lag between general experience and its interpretation. We shall now explore what this means more specifically in terms of the developmental limits evident in the growing child.

INTELLECTUAL IMMATURITY

To interpret what happens to him and what his experiences have to say to him, a child develops powers of thought. In his early years this occurs through sensory perception and the power to recognise objects in the world around him. The growth of language in the second year of life enables him to name the objects he recognises, thus further widening his powers of thought. He is able more and more to remember his experiences and to recall events and objects no longer present. The raw material for what we loosely call the development of intelligence is present but there is still a long period to go before the child can think clearly, logically and accurately.

In the pre-school years and in the first years in school, there are several intellectual limitations evident in children which obviously restrict their thinking. One of these is the egocentric nature of childish thought. The child's world is centred round himself and experiences cannot be objectively understood, only in relation to what is directly happening 'here and now to me'. Some time ago I had occasion to transport a small child Karen to nursery school and each morning we saw the distant university clock tower. As we got nearer to it we came down a hill and the tower appeared to sink out of sight. Karen watched this occurrence many times until one morning she said, 'Isn't it funny, that tower going up and down?' 'No, Karen,' I said, 'the tower doesn't go up and down. It's us going up and down the hill that does it. The tower still remains the same.' Long discussions followed which left Karen completely unconvinced. She

27

could not see the situation objectively because her thinking was firmly egocentric.

A further limitation at this time is the inability to relate one fact to another with any accuracy. The child is monofocal in his thinking, only able to deal with one fact at a time, and relational thinking develops only slowly and painfully. This makes for many faulty generalisations. Journeying by car with a five-year-old in Wales we pointed out the mountain Cader Idris. Several hours later the child pointed at Snowdon, saying in great excitement, 'There's Cader Idris again.' Although the shapes of the two mountains were obviously different, the child justified his statement because both mountains had a tiny wisp of cloud over the summit. Children often fix upon an irrelevancy like this as the basis of their reasoning, and it is not surprising that their generalisations are faulty.

Finally, when very young children have arrived at their conclusions they have no intellectual check on whether they are mistaken or not. As adults we try to revise our thinking to see if our ideas are consistent. Young children seem unable to do this, moving only forward in their thought with charming but misguided assurance. This explains children's difficulties in checking arithmetical sums, most of them finding that subtraction as a reversible form of addition a perplexing idea to grasp.

Egocentric, single focus and irreversible thinking are symptomatic of what Piaget calls pre-operational or intuitive thought. Research evidence indicates that in religious thinking this continues to at least 7 or 8 years in most children.

The period of childhood covered roughly by the

junior school years sees the next major step in intellectual development. The child becomes less egocentric in his thinking, learns in certain experiences to check on his conclusions by reversing his thought and begins to relate different facts and features of a situation together. His generalisations are less frequently faulty and thought becomes reasonably objective. It is conceded that the university tower does not go up and down and is static all the time. Its shape, size and position are not dependent on the position of people looking at it. Cader Idris is no longer confused with Snowdon because irrelevancies such as clouds are disregarded and more essential features are recognised as important. In arithmetic sums can be checked by simple reversible procedures.

Yet immaturities remain which still impede the child's thinking. This continuing limitation is due to the child's restriction of thought to concrete situations, visual experience and data apprehended through sensory activity. Talk in abstract generalisations to children at this stage, and they will try to translate it into concrete terms, often with considerable inaccuracy. A father came home to find the walls of the newly-decorated lounge scribbled on by the children. Having chastised them and warned them not to write on walls again, he came back the next evening and found them scribbling on the bedroom walls. When confronted with their crime they were genuinely distressed, because they had thought the scribbling veto only applied to 'downstairs rooms where you sit'. We all know that specific instructions, concrete experience and tangible, factual materials should be used in the junior years. The use of general terms and abstract ideas will lead to difficulties simply because concrete elements will tend to dominate the pupil's thinking.

Religious experience, expressed in many biblical passages, is often very abstract, non-concrete and frequently depends upon subtle play upon words. Love, goodness, holiness, spirit are only a few examples of abstract ideas used in religious education; and where the child translates these into concrete ideas there is frequent misunderstanding and perversion of what is intended. As we shall see later, this affects the child's religious concepts, especially the mental pictures he forms of God. The frequency with which God is described in the Bible in human terms fixes in children's minds the man-likeness of God and this anthropomorphism, natural to the child, is taken literally. God is not thought of *as* a man, but he *is* a man. He is most frequently depicted by children as a very old man with a long white beard, sitting on the clouds, surrounded by angels and clad in appropriate Palestinian garments. How God operates in the universe is seen physically and concretely, often the very opposite to the spiritual truths of which the New Testament speaks.

This stage of concrete operational thinking poses the greatest intellectual problem for children seeking to understand religion. It is largely responsible for Peter's ideas of a sub-religious character, which are often in contradiction with the essential nature of Christianity. There is strong and disturbing evidence to indicate that a great deal of religious teaching merely reinforces crude, sub-religious thought in junior children. Their imprisonment within concrete concepts and their frequent literalisms make it difficult for them to step forward into a more spiritual understanding of religious truth.

Intellectual maturing into a stage we might call abstract operational thinking, liberates most pre-adolescents from the childhood limitations I have outlined. How and why this happens and what pressures of experience are responsible for this we cannot tell. We do know that the capacity to deal with ideas of a more abstract nature tends to develop during the second to third year of secondary schooling. Verbal propositions can be treated at a higher, non-concrete level and symbolic thinking, so very important for religious understanding, now becomes possible. In science this means that the setting up of hypotheses can be used, so that instead of starting with facts the pupil can begin with a theory or hypothesis and test the facts against the theory. This type of hypothetical thinking is just as important for forming a theology as it is for physical science.

We can now see more clearly the processes of thought which are partly responsible for the child's intellectual limitations, and which influence the very young towards a pre-religious and the junior children towards a sub-religious mode of thinking. This is treated in more detail elsewhere,[3] but we need now to examine other limiting factors which we have tended to underestimate in religious education.

LINGUISTIC LIMITATIONS

During their early childhood children acquire a large and ever-growing vocabulary. All investigations show with striking similarity that in various areas of experience a child's use of words far outstrips his understanding. It is, of course, by using words frequently that a

31

child grasps their true meaning, and in what context it is appropriate to use particular words. But adults, not least teachers, are frequently misled by their verbal fluency into believing that children understand more than they actually do. Words may be acquired merely by hearing them spoken repeatedly, and it is possible to use words while their significance is not really grasped.

Where religion is concerned, children soon acquire a religious vocabulary, often used with fluency and skill, most of which in the early years is not rooted in any understanding of their real truth. The child who comes home from the vicarage and states 'I've just had tea with God' is using a word he dimly associates with Sundays, churches, services and vicars in the wrong context. The confused 'Lead us not into Thames Station' is an attempt to make what is apparently confusing into a more sensible sentence in the Lord's Prayer.

Religious language is absorbed by children naturally as they encounter it in their experience, by overhearing conversation, by attending church services or school assemblies, and by other means. They can also acquire it by adults deliberately conditioning them to it, as in the teaching of a catechism by rote. In some churches catechetical teaching is highly regarded and is thought to be effective. If it takes place alongside relevant experience and enlightened teaching it may have a limited use. In my view it is analagous to teaching the multiplication tables before the child has had enough experience of counting, measuring and forming number bonds which build the foundations of number concepts. Catechetical teaching, with its rote-memorised answers, certainly builds up a religious vocabulary, as multiplication tables are successful in building a number vocabulary. In both cases it is vocabulary with little conceptual substance, and may lead to the illusion that something of greater value is being taught.

The danger is very real in religious education, because religious language is secondary language using analogy, metaphor, simile and other devices to communicate the nature of God. To understand this language we must first be able to comprehend the experience upon which the analogy, metaphor or simile is based. When a sentence such as 'The Lord is my shepherd' is used, we try to convey the care and love of God by the analogy of a shepherd caring for his sheep. The helplessness of sheep, the value of each in the shepherd's eyes, the sacrifice he may have to make for the sheep, are all experiences of which we must be aware if the analogy is to convey any meaning at all. 'I am the light of the world' carries a great variety of metaphorical meaning, and we must be able to recall many different images of light that guides us, calms our fears, searches out hidden places, burns up waste, exposes and purifies before we can grasp what Jesus was saying.

Once we have come to terms with this basic fact about religious language we recognise it more as the language of poetry than matter of fact language. To teach it, therefore, by rote is more nonsensical than teaching a number vocabulary, since to take religious language at its face value, in a literal sense as children will tend to do, only creates confusion and difficulties where they need not exist. The answer is partly to use language which is simple and appropriate for children, but more importantly to stimulate a wide range of experience which will enrich a child's view of life, so that the impact of religious language will not be made in a vacuum, but will be lit up by accumulated experience. No religious teaching should occur without a constant cross-reference to what a child has known and encountered for himself. For this reason we must turn now to the world of a child's experience and see why and where this enrichment is necessary before religious development can occur.

RESTRICTED EXPERIENCE OF CHILDREN

The younger the child the less extensive will be his experience of life. This in itself explains many of the immature judgments children make about varied problems, situations and people. Their innocent and rather naïve assumptions about all kinds of things make them both endearing and exasperating creatures to live with. Many experiences have come their way, some being encountered at a very superficial level. Yet continually children use all their experiences in building up their concepts, attitudes and beliefs into complex systems.

The restricted experience of children may be due to one of two factors. One is the fact of not having lived long enough, and the other the lack of opportunity that the environment imposes. Let us look at these two restrictive elements separately.

Children need time to explore their world, to come to terms with it and to grow alongside what they know. For this reason the child's natural egocentricity restricts him simply because he has no other experience to go on. As he meets other children at play, and later in school, he experiences the strains and stresses of personal relationships. Friendships involve not only getting but giving also, and by such demands on him a child's experiences of people mature. His social experience is therefore of first importance, not only for teaching him how to be a human being but also to reflect upon what it means to be human. Children only slowly and gradually, through their self-concepts, through concepts of parents, friends and enemies and similar ideas, move towards a mature understanding of human life.

Yet until some such reflection at a personal level is achieved, the major insights of the Christian faith cannot be grasped. The key to the relationship of love between man and God, and between man and man is in the hands of the child who has experienced what it is to be loved, or to have lost love, who has come face to face with himself in the demands of social living. Deeper still is the experience of redemptive need, to be saved from oneself and a realistic awareness of one's own nature. It is the sheer moral inexperience of the young which makes them unaware of the real issues of life.

Awareness of time itself moves from an immature idea to more mature concepts as children grow older. In terms of a span of time young children appear to have no notion of how long an hour or a day is. It is only gradually that they acquire both a time sense and a time-reading skill. As their span of comprehended time increases so does their idea of sequence in time. For the young child time appears to be disjointed, having no coherent sequence. What we may loosely call a historical time sense is still relatively undeveloped by the time pupils move up into secondary schools. We should reflect upon these facts when we consider the historical sequences assumed in many current religious syllabuses for children in the primary school.

Time, of course, is often measured in terms of space, how long it takes to travel the distance between two places. A child's judgment of distance will obviously be limited by the amount of travelling he has done. The longer he lives the further afield he explores. In these days of affluence more and more children are travelling more frequently than before. It is possible that spatial concepts will mature more quickly than in previous times and that the modern child's grasp of geographical concepts will consequently improve more quickly. Yet we should consider the implications of this for teaching religious stories embedded in a particular time and place. Fairly typical is the idea of a Lancashire child of nine that Jerusalem is a few miles south of Oldham. I do not think there was any conscious reference here to Blake's 'satanic mills'!

So much for experience limited by the age of children. Some of these experiences can be limited by the lack of opportunity offered by the environment. Children having no social experience with other children, poor relationships with parents, little opportunity to explore their world actively and eagerly, and who never travel beyond their locality will take longer to mature in the areas of life we have discussed. But there are other restrictions imposed upon all the children of a particular environment by what I would call the limitations of the culture.

Because a great deal of religious education material deals with ancient biblical civilisation it is relevant to compare it with the culture in which modern children are reared. To use a shorthand term, 'bible-society', we can see that it was a predominantly rural civilisation, composed partly of settled agricultural communities and partly of nomadic groups. Communities were small in size and even the larger cities such as Jerusalem rather resembled overgrown villages, retaining face-to-face relationships and some personal intimacy. The teaching of the Old and New Testaments reflect the values, cultures and essentially the rural nature of this civilisation.

The majority of children in Britain today live in a society with very few similarities to bible-society. They are members of mainly urban groups, most of them living in large residential or industrial areas. Mass production manufacture rather than rural occupations are the rule. In large cities the intimacy of small groups is frequently lost and where the Bible speaks in the experience of the countryside it is a countryside of vastly different climate and character to that known by a twentieth-century British child.

A further social difference is the contrast between a society which was pre-scientific in its assumptions (one major assumption being a belief in the supernatural) and a modern society where science and technology influence everything in our culture. Our children are reared within a critical, rational and questioning culture which begins to affect their world view from an earlier age than we have realised. The fruits of technology, seen in a greatly increased standard of living, appears to have been accompanied by an absorption in material prosperity and a growing indifference to spiritual matters.

Confirmation of this gap of experience can be seen in research results where children tend to regard the Bible as a supernatural book, dealing with holy people in a holy land, clad in special holy clothes, all in a special holy period of time. This remoteness of bible-society also encourages adolescents to dismiss biblical teaching as irrelevant since the experience, language, imagery and assumptions appear to be so vastly different from their own in the twentieth century. One of our major tasks in education is to bridge this cultural gap, so that the experience of which the Bible speaks, although expressed within the context of a vastly different society, is still seen as the basic experience of men and women of all times and societies, including our own. It is doubtful whether this can be readily understood as a general principle, because of intellectual limitations, much before the time of early adolescence.

THE IMPLICATIONS

The intellectual immaturity of children, their linguistic limitations and their restricted experience, both personal and cultural, does not mean that religious education in the early years of development must be abandoned. Some religious truths may be known without a young person achieving a high level of abstract reasoning. Language when used wisely and at the right level need not be a barrier to understanding. New experiences may be stimulated and past experiences reorganised in an intelligent programme of Christian education, which prepares children for the succeeding stages in their development, as well as answering the spiritual needs of the moment.

A realistic recognition of the limitations of immaturity discussed in this chapter is vital if we are to devise a programme which meets the religious needs of the young. Once we have made this recognition we can work within the limitations which research and general observation indicate. The sum total of the findings is that a great amount of biblical material as used at present is inappropriate, especially systematic historical teaching, before secondary schooling. Even where it is appropriate, a more realistic choice must be made in devising syllabuses to meet the intellectual needs of adolescents to prepare them for the period of questioning and doubt which lies ahead. The emphasis should be placed more and more upon using the natural experience of children so that the religious nature of that experience shall be known and placed alongside the experience of others, both in the past and the present.

In the next chapter we will address ourselves to the positive aspect of the question, for what kind of religious teaching and experience are our pupils ready at the varying stages of their development?

4

What is Readiness for Religion?

DESPITE THE LIMITATIONS outlined in the last
chapter, it is clear that children are interested in religion. They display real insights into spiritual matters
from time to time and appear to involve themselves in
prayer, religious services and other activities with great
seriousness. If religion may be defined as 'the feelings,
acts and experiences of individual(s) ... so far as they
apprehend themselves to stand in relation to whatever
they may consider the divine',[4] it is plain that children
in our own culture from late infancy onwards are religious. It is also plain that the religion of which they
are capable at the age of seven years is not the religion
of which they are capable at seventeen or twenty-seven.
By the very nature of the young child, he is crude,
immature and naïve in his religious beliefs.

This is why I have characterised, from research evidence available, three stages of development, named pre-
religious, sub-religious and religious. In our culture even
very young children accept the existence of 'the divine',
frequently an amalgam of ideal parent figures and
Father Christmas rolled into one. The young child also
feels himself to have a relationship with this 'divine
being', even if it is the curious merging of primitive
animistic religion and a trusting, more mature relationship.

What is Readiness for Religion?

When I say that children are ready for religion from an early age, this must therefore be qualified in terms of what kind of religion they are ready for. Christianity is not only a faith difficult for adult men and women to understand and accept, but it is also one of the world's most advanced religions, in the level of theological thought demanded. It would be much easier, for example, to teach children certain aspects of Hinduism, with its animistic assertions, its many gods and its pantheistic theology. To teach the Christian faith 'pure and undefiled' in an adult form to children is impossible because it is unrealistic. Do we then dilute Christian teaching, or teach some aspects of the Old Testament because it appears to resemble the more primitive ideas of children in the primary school? Is it possible to build up gradually a general understanding of what Christians believe? If so, what aspects of Christianity are children ready to learn at certain stages in their development?

Before we can attempt any answer to fundamental questions of this kind I want first to examine what is meant by 'readiness', to illustrate it from other areas of learning, and then to see how this applies to the teaching of religion.

READINESS FOR LEARNING

We have long been familiar with such phrases as reading readiness, writing readiness and more recently, number readiness. These phrases mean that children have arrived at a suitable stage when they can begin to learn the particular skills of reading, writing and number. This concept of readiness for learning involves a number of inter-related assumptions which teachers implement in practice, sometimes without being consciously aware of them.

The first assumption is that there is a time in development when the maturing of a child allows skills to be learned, previously impossible, because the necessary physical co-ordination was lacking, intellectual powers were inadequate or the child was emotionally unready, in that he was uninterested and unmotivated regarding the skill to be learned. In some skills physical readiness is more important than intellectual readiness, and in others it is intellectual readiness which appears to be dominant. In all skills to be learned a child must be adequately motivated; so that some measure of readiness is necessary in all three areas of development.

Not only does this assumption mean that there is a time for each child when he is most ready to begin a certain skill, it also means a concept of readiness in continuing the skill to higher and higher levels of complexity. What we may call incremental stages in learning have to be systematised, as in reading when the spoken identification of objects in the classroom leads to labelling of the objects, which in turn leads to identification by flash-cards, which in turn leads to simple reading books, and then an incremental increase in vocabulary so that more and more complex reading material can be understood. Good reading books exploit a child's natural interests, use vocabulary natural to him and relate experiences familiar to the child.

A further assumption involved in readiness for learning is that we do not wait passively for children to grow into readiness, but we can actively assist the process of readiness by suitable preparatory learning. In developing the skill of writing, varied experiences of scribbling, drawing and painting help the child more and more to control his hand movements. The eye and hand co-ordinations necessary for a writing skill to develop may at a later stage be assisted by such exercises as those devised by Marion Richardson. Wise teachers will select and systematically introduce their children to preliminary experience relevant to the learning of the new skill.

It will be seen, therefore, that readiness for learning is not concerned merely with the specific time of the beginning of a skill, but also with what precedes it and what follows it. This concept involves the whole of the sequence of learning.

Much more evidence is needed, but there is sufficient available for us to suggest that certain religious truths may be ripe to develop at certain moments of readiness in a child's growth. The limitations I have outlined show us what kind of learning is not possible at certain stages; that is, what the children are not ready to receive. These in themselves are indicators to what is possible, and the key may lie more in the realm of emotion than intellect in the first decade of development.

Incremental stages in religious teaching should reflect the child's increasing capacity to deal with religious ideas of increasing complexity. Until now syllabuses have been largely concerned to increase the quantity of religious material with increasing age, instead of the quality. Further, it is not possible to say that at such an age a child is ready to learn the doctrine of the holy spirit or truths about the nature of the church. This is to oversimplify the whole idea. It is possible that some aspects of the holy spirit or the church may be within the reach of a child's understanding at a certain stage, principally because he has certain personal experiences which he can place alongside what is taught. Sound religious teaching will exploit a child's natural interest rather than impose upon him an artificial and irrelevant series of ideas. It will also use vocabulary natural to the child, not an adult form of words difficult for him to grasp.

Waiting passively for readiness to develop is no part of the function of the religious teacher. Many could well be less zealous and more patient, since undue and unsuitable pressures can set up negative attitudes as in other subjects. But active preparation which enriches, directs and stimulates relevant experience may be the most important function for infant school teachers in religious education. This preliminary experience is the foundation upon which the later teaching is based, but all too frequently in the past we have been so eager to get on with 'the real teaching of the gospel' that inadequate foundations have been laid. Without this valuable initial work, much of what is taught may result in a mere religious vocabulary or the crystallising of ideas too soon, which prevents a child reaching forward to higher levels of thought. Far from helping the child, we impede his religious growth. To quote only one example, the young child who, after hearing the parable of the Prodigal Son, said, 'I do think his Daddy might have gone with him!' The distortion is complete, for instead of hearing the story of a loving father, he had heard the story of a neglectful one.[5]

We shall now explore what intellectual, emotional and physical readiness may mean for religious education.

INTELLECTUAL READINESS

Powers of thought develop in a fairly predictable sequence. First, there is sensory experience of the world, through seeing, hearing, touching, smelling, tasting and total body sensations. Very soon the child begins to select from the thousands of sensations he receives and so controls their impact, choosing what is important to him. This is the process of perception, so that what is seen is not always what is perceived. The child in a moment of time will be receiving many sensations but only a few will be perceived. From the several objects and colours on his pram cover one may dominate, namely the yellow ball he enjoys handling, sucking and generally exploring. Perception is the process of recognition and leads to the naming of experience. There then follows conceptualisation, the drawing together of similar classes of experiences. A child may perceive the figure of mother, observe the things she does and also, as his horizons widen, see how other mothers behave, until a concept of mother or motherhood develops. At first the concept will be very crude and partial because of limited experience and a natural egocentric view of life, and only gradually will more objective and more sophisticated concepts of motherhood be achieved.

By the time the child begins school he will have several hundred concepts, the fruits of his perceptive experience, which act as a guide to his intellectual activity. Most of these will be concerned with home, parents, other children, his physical environment, his toys, his diet, his clothes, the sky, the sun and the moon, water, soil, sand and the myriad materials he encounters daily. Perhaps the most important concept he makes, which affects all other concepts, is the self-concept; how he regards himself and the general way he assesses his own worth. This later becomes a starting point for most of the important religious concepts he will need in order to understand the Christian faith.

Alongside these concepts, feeding them and sometimes impeding them, is the growth of the child's vocabulary. As we have seen, children may use many words for which they have no adequate conceptual thought. Words are exciting material to experiment with and they are tried out in various contexts, even though there will be no adequate meaning attached to them. They may be used simply because a child likes the sounds. It is fundamental, therefore, that children acquire a suitable conceptual basis for the words they use, namely that words should summarise for children their own generalised experience.

In the pre-school and during the early schooling years, concepts are extremely inaccurate due to the pre-operational nature of the child's thinking. This means that children arrive at mistaken conclusions because often minor details of an experience dominate the child's thinking, or the wrong associations are made. In the story of the Temptations, children frequently explain that Jesus would not turn stone into bread, because 'Jesus said he had not to eat bread alone'. This was further explained that 'by bread alone' meant 'They should have something else like cheese and something to drink'. The young child returning from tea at the vicarage and announcing that he has 'had tea with God' has a similar conceptual problem.[6]

This is why I have called this stage of children's

thinking pre-religious, in an intellectual and conceptual sense. They find it difficult to conceptualise religious truth without distorting it when faced with formal teaching, however attractive and interesting some Bible stories may be. Children at this stage are ready to receive unrelated experiences of life. Everything is a source of wonder, and 'the religious' character of everyday experience seems to be the most natural way to prepare them. This calls for a much more indirect method of religious education in which the wonder of God's world in nature, animals, the sky and all experiences which come naturally to him can be surrounded by the assumption, often unspoken by the teacher, that all this is part of the divine creation. In short, little can be taught effectively which is foreign to the child and which does not arise naturally from his experience.

Children who have achieved operational thinking at the concrete level begin to form more realistic concepts, although these are restricted to observable and concrete facts. Intellectually, therefore, they appear to be ready to absorb a great deal of data and at the same time develop the ability to relate these facts together. This is why themes based upon their own experience which will provide a related view of life and which offer a religious interpretation appear to meet the needs of junior children much more than imposing religious or biblical teachings unrelated to their real world. Immature concepts of time make systematic and chronological teaching of biblical events unsatisfactory, but juniors can and do relate all the knowledge they acquire to their life experience. I have characterised this period as the sub-religious stage intellectually, since the more spiritual truths of Christianity are frequently reduced to

47

pre-Christian concepts. I use the term sub-religious as synonymous with pre-Christian.

Life-themes appropriate for early juniors, such as Our homes, People who help us, Shepherds and their sheep, and many others, have a threefold intellectual purpose. First of all, they include 'religious' teaching in all other areas of learning and do not seal it off as something separate and therefore irrelevant. Secondly, religion is the frame of reference within which all other knowledge can be seen and to which it can be related. Thirdly, by using what the child knows and what he can explore for himself at first hand, religious education is being experienced at a concrete level and concepts can be formed which are not distortions. This would also seem to be an appropriate time for pupils to explore bible-lands and bible-society in the sense that they can learn some of the background facts about the way of life within which Jesus lived and taught. Much of the misunderstanding of later biblical teaching appears to stem from an unfamiliarity with the geographical and social nature of Palestine.

By the late junior years and the first year of secondary schooling, the period of pre-adolescence, our pupils are becoming less concrete minded and are becoming dissatisfied with their concrete limitations. They reveal an intermediate stage between concrete and fully adult operational thinking. They are almost ready for what I would call a fully religious conceptual teaching, but only of a fairly straightforward kind. Biblical material can now be looked at more systematically and the study of a simple life of Christ begun. Even so, such a study is a study of events and people, rather than having a significance couched in abstract terms. Historical thinking still appears to be too immature for the study of the Old Testament on a chronological basis. Alongside the beginnings of New Testament teaching, life-themes based upon the pupils' experience should continue and no opportunity should be lost in relating the experience of people in New Testament times to personal experience.

The change from concrete to abstract modes of thought appears to become possible in religious thinking about the age of thirteen years. The adolescent is now in what I would call his religious stage of development, in which he is intellectually ready to apprehend what is the Christian faith. Its concepts are now within the grasp of his intellect and experience, although he has still far to go in his religious search. But if at least by the time he enters the adult life of work he has some objective knowledge of what Christians believe, he is then able to accept or reject these beliefs at a genuinely personal level.

It is not only intellectual maturing which makes a fuller teaching possible, but also the accumulation of varied experiences which underlie the great spiritual questions raised by Christianity. As these are mainly highly charged with emotion, such as a sense of insecurity and a developing moral sensitivity, we shall look at them in more detail when we consider emotional readiness. It is enough to say that if the basic theme of religion is redemption, those to whom it must appeal should have had some first-hand experience of that from which religion claims to redeem them. In short, sin, death, frustration, enmity, lack of purpose, weakness, must have been known in some measure at first-hand if anyone is to feel the need to be saved from them. To put it in another way, we need to have lived long enough to have experienced the real problems of the human condition before we see the point of what religion offers. With childhood receding, the awakening adolescent is becoming aware of what it means to be an adult for the first time, and this creates, intellectually and emotionally, a readiness for adult religion.

EMOTIONAL READINESS

Children are highly motivated in relation to religion. Although many children find long religious services a bore, loud organ music frightening and a great deal of religious language incomprehensible, they are well disposed in their early years towards religion and religious teaching. What surprises many people is that these positive attitudes slowly move towards indifference in many adolescents, if not towards more negative and hostile feelings, about Christianity. At a time when religion intellectually can mean something really relevant in the lives of young people, the willingness to think strenuously about it seems to die. There is much evidence to show that their quest for meaning, their search for answers to their problems and a spiritual hunger still continues. It is 'religion', as the official teaching of school and church, which is rejected. There are unmistakable indications that both the content and methods of religious education may aggravate, if not actually cause, this tragic situation.

Belief in God is basically a willingness to trust. It is not primarily a matter of the intellect but of the emotions. In this sense a new-born baby is ready for religion in that his entire life is dependent upon a power beyond himself. The baby does not have to learn to trust, he does so naturally and by necessity, and the power beyond himself on whom he is dependent is initially his mother. The child feels secure with mother, and at a much later time, with father. Any disruption of the relationship with mother, the major figure in his early development, leads to insecurity which can have far-reaching and disturbing results.[7] A mother, or a mother-substitute, someone with whom the child can have a continuous relationship, seems to supply these emotional vitamins, just as a baby requires physical vitamins, and is a condition for healthy emotional development.

From our knowledge of the young child, we know that parents are regarded in divine terms. They are endowed with the qualities of omnipotence, omniscience and even omnipresence. It is natural that parents are regarded as all-powerful by their young children and only slowly do they become aware that mother or father are not in full control. If a parent falls ill or dies, this comes as a great shock to children whose fantasies are quickly shaken. Most children cannot think of a situation when parents are not available for help, and so ideas of omnipresence are again natural. Many children, when doing what they know is forbidden, have an uneasy feeling that a parent is watching. It takes a considerable time for children to know that this is an incorrect feeling. Similarly with knowledge, children feel that the powerful people whom they trust so completely know everything there is to know about everything.

This godlike image of parents is shattered for all children, sooner or later. Bovet comments succinctly on the significance of this for religion, 'From deifying his parents, the child turns to parentalising the deity.' I do not wish to enter into a discussion here of the Freudian view that religion is merely a projection of infantile desires, but merely underline that belief in God is rooted in the parental relationship, and that children turn to God naturally as they do to a good parent. I shall return to a fuller discussion of this in a later chapter.

Vestiges of these divine qualities spread beyond parents to all the adult world, especially to such people as teachers, ministers and clergy, policemen and those seen by children to possess some visible authority. In an increasingly secular society it is surprising that so many children automatically assume that adults generally believe in God. This illusion gradually breaks down, but there is an unexpected delay, almost into adolescence, before most of our pupils become aware that not everyone is religious nor believes in God. This, in part, may explain children's eagerness to learn about religion because it seems to please the adults around them. Unconsciously, many parents, who have long since ceased to care about religion, appear to hesitate about disillusioning their children. Perhaps they themselves still yearn for the innocent and simple faith of childhood, now lost, and recaptured nostalgically through their children at times such as Christmas. This is often interpreted as deception by young adolescents, and may be part of the cynicism about adults which some young people so vigorously express.

Emotional identification with Christian beliefs, then, is the norm through British primary schools, and we must beware of exploiting this eagerness unfairly. It can so easily be misinterpreted by teachers as the time most suitable for religious teaching of an intellectual kind.

What is most interesting is that in the first years of schooling children fantasise their way into religion, rather than think their way into it intellectually. Since their intellectual ideas are limited, children seem to compensate by playing, dramatising, thinking imaginatively and through creative expression. What they find difficult through words and intellect, they explore more easily through feeling and imagination. What some have called the fairy-tale stage of religion seems to extend well into the junior school and in some way religious education must use this playful way of looking at life for the benefit of their children.

In addition to all this, emotionally children in primary schools look at knowledge as all of a piece, and they find religious teachings about people of long ago in a far-off land rather artificial. It creates in their minds a dualistic world view, which becomes very evident in secondary schooling, that there is one world called 'religious' and the other called 'scientific'. The first has to do with holy things, holy people in holy clothes, dealing with holy happenings in a Holy land (why on earth do we label maps with this inappropriate title?) and on some occasions taught by a holy teacher in a holy room. In this kind of world God *was* present, moving about the physical world organising thunderstorms, interfering with battles and generally behaving unpredictably. The second is the modern world they know of, with cars, central heating and television, in which thunderstorms can be explained by natural laws, and about which they try to think logically.

The evidence, in my view, indicates this rift by the end of the junior school, and becomes more vocally expressed by the third year of secondary schooling, when some science teaching has been experienced and a more rigorous operational mode of thinking develops. The reasons are, I believe, as much emotional as intellectual. Since the content of religious syllabuses tends to be overwhelmingly in the form of bible narrative, pupils hear the same material many times. At a time when most of it could evoke a significant response and have a fresh impact when placed alongside their experience, it is received in a jaded and bored manner.

Another reason for the beginnings of negative attitudes in early adolescence is a growing critical turn of mind. Having, by their own natural disposition, distorted Bible stories into literal truths they do not convey, they now perplexingly turn round and condemn a great deal of religious education as 'childish'. To be sure, this is all part of the grand gesture of becoming more grown up, but there seems to be more to it than this. The major ingredient seems to be the way in which they have been taught to regard the Bible, almost superstitiously, as a monolithic body of unquestioned truth. By making them, often unintentionally, into premature fundamentalists, we have sown the seeds of rejection. The tragedy is that their rejection is based upon a gross misconception, before they have been exposed to what is the true nature of the Bible. It is evident therefore that we must actively teach them to exercise critical thinking about the Bible while they are within the context of belief. If we do not they will exercise critical thinking outside it and invariably will reject religion on 'childish' grounds.

A final reason for negative feelings about religion in adolescence seems to be not only the content of teaching, but the way in which it is taught. Young people seem to resent authoritarian teaching and more and more wish to explore ideas and beliefs for themselves. Good permissive relationships, allowing personal questioning and discussion, seem to be the best climate for religious education in secondary schools. In these days when adolescents are concerned about their status, we should stop thinking of them as children, and address them as young people. This would be a beginning. But a more radical change of teaching content and method is needed, if adolescents, who are searching hungrily for truth, are to turn to Christianity as a fulfilment of their emotional as well as their intellectual needs.

Emotional readiness for religion is noted by all research dealing with adolescence. Summarising these researches, Michael Argyle[8] says, 'It is the age of religious awakening, during which time people either become converted or decide to abandon the faith of their childhood, if they had one.' Emotionally, therefore, as well as intellectually, adolescence is the age at which there is the greatest religious potential.

PHYSICAL READINESS

Religious learning does not directly require a state of physical readiness, in the same way as learning a physical skill, or a literacy skill, such as reading or writing. Nevertheless, this factor is relevant both directly and indirectly.

A great amount of religious education involves reading and it is evident that children find the Bible physically a difficult book to read. Small print, the format of the page into two columns and usually devoid of illustrations, as well as the archaic language, repel children in an age when they are used to colourful attractive reading books, well-illustrated, couched in a vocabulary at their level. The invention of school bibles or the use of modern versions may help, but what is needed is the presentation of religious materials, sometimes using biblical sources, sometimes not, more in accord with the reading skills of primary school pupils. In the 'Readiness for Religion' series my colleagues and I are hoping to meet the problem. Although many more attractive textbooks are now available for secondary schools, materials more appropriate to adolescents are needed, especially for average to backward pupils in secondary modern schools. Many books for adolescents also tend to be fundamentalist in nature, if not in intention. Books about the Bible which are provocative of critical and creative thoughts are very rare indeed.

Drawing and writing are frequently recommended in day and Sunday schools, as activities for all ages of pupils. Often we do not consider whether these activities are appropriate for the actual pupils we teach. Younger children love to draw and are blissfully untroubled by the inaccuracies of their artistic efforts. Many older children and adolescents become so self-conscious that their work is poor. Care should be taken to provide a wide range of choice in the kind of activities recommended. Moreover, the telling of a Bible story and 'expression work' afterwards is a traditional method we should consider. Later, I shall be suggesting alternatives, which in the light of what we know about religious development, seem to be more suitable 'activities'.

Less directly relevant, if we think of religious education in too narrow a manner, is the development of the

56

young in terms of physical confidence. Some children are lacking in this confidence, avoiding the physical challenge of some new activity, and are afraid to be physically adventurous. At its roots this is a state of emotional unreadiness. The fear which impedes physical achievement is a spiritual condition, for such a child cannot trust himself or his environment enough to let go and venture into the unknown. This is an unnatural condition, since all children are adventurous; it is part of their natural drive to explore and try out new activities.

Within the limits of safety, as part of their growth as persons, such children should be encouraged to take part in activities which foster physical confidence. Such is the close interplay between body, mind and spirit that this could contribute to their religious education; that is, their development towards confident relationships with their fellows and with God. It is significant that religious syllabuses tend to think of religious education as a purely cerebral activity. Children and adolescents so enjoy the movement of the body and demanding physical activities, that there should surely be some place for this kind of experience in Christian education. In a movement such as Outward Bound, adolescents are faced, through physical challenge, with themselves, and what is loosely called character education is the aim. More and more this kind of challenge is spreading through youth clubs and other youth organisations. We should see the need to have similar suitable physical challenges for children. Perhaps this would help us to be aware that physical education is of spiritual significance by building up a person who has sufficient confidence to trust himself and God.

5

What We Should Be Trying To Do

IT WILL SEEM a little odd that I have come so far without raising the all-important question of what should be the aims of Christian education. It makes sense to me to first of all outline what research over the past few years has to say to teachers, for in doing so all the major issues and problems involved in religious education have become clearer. We have gained a much more realistic picture of the nature of the pupils we teach, the limitations which affect their religious growth and the kind of religious teaching they appear to be ready to receive during their continuing development. Teachers of any subject must not expect their pupils to attain the impossible, and what is possible should play a decisive part in deciding our educational aims. In religious teaching this also makes educational sense, and the time has come to ask if what religious educators have been trying to do can in any way be made consistent with the developing needs of children and adolescents.

A number of the aims of Christian education are what might be called social, in that the intention is to improve the moral or spiritual climate of our society. Much of the inspiration for the religious settlement of 1944 emerged from a period in wartime when our democratic society needed a dynamic sense of national purpose with which to confront totalitarian ideologies. There is no doubt that the intentions of our legislators were predominently social at that time; namely that the Christian religion could provide a purpose and an ethic which the whole nation could share. It was not thought that introducing religion into our state system would make a Christian nation, or that the vast majority would return to church allegiance that they had long ago lost. It was thought, however, that the values implicit within the Christian faith would act as a kind of moral, cultural and social binding force which would form an important foundation for our democracy.

My view is that these social aims are secondary aims, and that if Christian education does result in such socially desirable ends they are to be welcomed. But to focus these as primary aims is to merely use religion as a pew-fodder, citizenship-fodder, and democracy-fodder device, which completely contradicts the teachings of Christ himself. Christianity should be taught because it is true, because it answers the deepest needs of human nature, and without a knowledge of the love of God and a relationship with him men and women will live impoverished lives.

This is not to dismiss the social aims in the teaching of religion, but merely to see them in their proper perspective. For this reason, we shall look at several social arguments briefly before we proceed to the more basic purpose of religious education.

THE MORAL ARGUMENT

It is a common view that religion and morals are closely related, morals stemming directly from the values believed in an accepted religious faith. If, for example, we believe in God and this belief involves the value of love for God and our fellow men, we would expect a person's behaviour to be more sensitive to the needs of others, to be more considerate, that is, more consistent with the command that we should love one another. There is a sense in which this is true, because a relationship with God should provide a moral purpose and a moral power to implement it. An essential part of Christian belief is that what makes a man a human being is his moral dilemma and his need to be redeemed or saved from his own dual nature.

Yet to use religion directly as a means of teaching moral values is to start the wrong way round. We start with the nature of the world we live in, the nature of human life, the nature of God and what kind of relationship he has with us. The centre of this is the fact of love. From this fact stems the whole of the life, teaching and redemptive life and death of Christ. In this sense Augustine's saying 'Love God and do as you like' is good morality, for if the implication of love is followed, then all that we do will be consistent with love.

The situation is often confused by what, in my view, is mis-named Christian Ethics. There is *a* Christian Ethic, which is the law of love, but there is no system of ethics laying down specific commands for each situation or human problem we encounter. Taken merely at the social level there is no Christian moral specific about war, divorce, family planning, or race relations, much though some of us would like such practical directives about these problems. Christians disagree among themselves on all these issues, and many more, because they have to interpret the meaning of the law of love in each situation. This is why Christianity, and especially Protestant Christianity, is so difficult. It offers a moral freedom of which many are afraid, and from which they will retreat into authoritarian moral negatives. The unfortunate image of churchgoers as 'against' so many enjoyable aspects of life is one expression of this situation. This is not an argument for a state of spiritual anarchy but for spiritual integrity. All I am trying to say is that moral specifics are by-products of religious faith. All the moral implications of Christian love can be, and often are, accepted by humanists. What is different for Christians is the ultimate source of their authority for loving, and the moral power that should flow from their belief in God.

Nevertheless, one of the needs of the young is to have standards of behaviour by which they can live. The psychological evidence available reveals that children live at the level of social necessity and social convenience, rather than at the behest of abstract exhortations. Their early standards are the results of parental, other adult, and later peer pressures. Sound moral development depends upon a fair measure of consistency between the behaviour of those whom children admire, and the standards they demand. True morality only begins to emerge when more personal moral choices are made, probably in early adolescence.

The major emphasis in Christian education, for more reasons than moral ones, should be upon the basis of moral authority; namely, belief in God and the nature of our relationship with him. If there is no emotional conviction that God is, that he is love, and that intellectually this is all of a piece with the whole of life, no appeal to religion as a moral authority is of any value. But the exploration of this belief, acting within its assumptions, and observing adults who apply a love relationship as parents, teachers and friends, appears to be a more realistic way of moral education than direct moral exhortation made within a religious context, of which the child has inadequate experience.

THE CULTURAL ARGUMENT

Another social aim often advanced for Christian education is that as part of the European culture, we are greatly indebted to the Judaeo-Christian tradition, and that to know our cultural heritage we must know something of these two religions and the society from which they sprang. The claim is often made that the true task of education is to confront each generation with its cultural heritage so that its inheritors can really understand the social context in which life is experienced, and reinterpret the culture in terms of their current needs. Perhaps this is one reason for the mass of biblical material recommended in most agreed syllabuses.

I readily accept the fact that the Judaeo-Christian tradition, embodied in the literature of the Bible, is a very important aspect of our culture. Many of our assumptions about marriage, democracy, civil and ecclesiastical law, individual rights and property, are based upon this tradition. Apart from religious considerations, to understand our society any educated person should have some comprehension of this area of knowledge.

There are two observations relevant to this aim that I want to make. The first is that it is a highly intellectual aim not realisable in childhood, since the kind of thinking demanded in an examination, comparison and discussion of these traditions, is more appropriate to late secondary schooling or higher education. Much propositional thought of a fairly high level (formal operational thinking) would be demanded, including a well-developed sense of historical sequence, time perspective and social experience. The second observation is that this aim can be dangerous encouragement to teach only a geography-history of Palestine. It reinforces the idea that religion is a series of facts to be known, an inculcation of information which may be called Scripture or Religious Knowledge, rather than religious education, which demands a much fuller view of its function in school and society.

What is of value in this aim is that before the message of the Bible can be understood, some realistic ideas of the society and people of the Bible must be grasped. For this reason we have included quite an amount of biblical social history in some of our children's materials. This is not studied in isolation but it is linked directly with children's experiences and their own society, as for example, in our Symbols Theme, where children explore the meaning of names, the symbolic use of number and stories in their own culture.

THE MISSIONARY ARGUMENT

Although it is illegal to teach 'any catechism or formulary of any particular religious denomination' (a requirement of the religious clauses of the 1944 Education Act) it is true to say that the Churches welcomed the Act as an expression of their missionary purpose. Our church and independent schools may teach their own denominational doctrine and actively encourage children in their schools to look forward to confirmation or church membership in a particular church. In the rest of our schools, however, a wider missionary opportunity is present, the aim of which is often expressed as 'growing Christians'. There is some truth in the view that this can only be effectively done by a Christian community through its own educational agencies, such as the Sunday school, and is impossible to do in such a secular community as a state school.

Yet, using 'church' in its widest sense, the day school, secular though it is, may be the only 'church' or religious community most children will directly experience. Attendance at a church is unknown to large numbers of our pupils, so that religious assembly at the beginning of each schoolday is the only service of worship they will know, and their religious knowledge classes the only religious teaching to which they will be exposed. This situation, welcomed by the churches, is hotly contested by small militant groups, such as the National Secular Society, who maintain that the vast majority of the nation has already voted with their feet in staying away from the churches. Nevertheless, few parents withdraw their children from religious education periods at school, as is their constitutional right.

Before a young person can decide to be a Christian he should understand what being a Christian means. I maintain that the major contribution of the day school teacher is to help his pupils to understand this at as deep a level, intellectually and emotionally, as possible. In this way a commitment to, or a rejection of, Christianity can be made *for the right reasons*. It is tragic for

64

an adolescent to be bulldozed into an emotional 'conversion' without a sound intellectual grasp of what he is letting himself in for. It is equally tragic for an adolescent to reject Christianity for infantile reasons, because he has not grasped the essential nature of the Christian faith nor the demands of Christ upon him.

The present weakness of Christian education is that the content and methods of teaching tend to encourage infantile decisions away from a Christian commitment. This is a direct result of trying to teach too much (and too much which is inappropriate) at too early an age. If we persist in this it reveals that we are more concerned for the needs of religion than the needs of the child. In a direct way we are doing religion a disservice also.

THE BASIS OF CHILDREN'S NEEDS

What I have called the social aims of religious education are only partially suitable, as I have tried to indicate when discussing the moral, cultural and missionary arguments. They are only valid in so far as they coincide with the personal needs of children and young people. To me, the basis of children's needs must be the starting point and the ultimate purpose of Christian education. Religion is eminently a personal search, a personal experience and a personal challenge. It is first and foremost a personal encounter with the divine. The aims of Christian education should therefore be directed towards the fulfilment of a child's personal needs as they are felt at the various stages of his development.

It follows from this that all really effective religious education stems, wherever possible, from the natural interests and activities of children, for these are the expression of their basic needs. Religion, therefore, as an interpretation of all that the child does, is bound up with every subject taught in school and cannot be segregated into one particular series of lessons on the timetable. The holding of 'religious' lessons, as something introduced from outside the child, is unnatural and contrary to the child's needs.

Ideally, then, we should follow and extend children's interests so that they come to see their experiences in depth. In such a setting religious truth as an interpretation of all experience is known not artificially but at a truly personal level. In this way religion and life are experienced as inseparable.

More and more teachers of the young are beginning to recognise this as a basic principle. But many are puzzled to know how it can be applied in the school and classroom situation. The suggestions I make in Part II are designed to help teachers towards the principle, summarised in what I call 'developmental religious education', based upon the needs of the growing child. I regard my suggestions, however, as merely a bridge across the gap between traditional Bible-centred aims and the emerging ideas of a more child-centred method.

When we talk about a child's basic needs, let me first of all dismiss the idea that a child has specifically religious needs. He needs religion, in its widest meaning, but he has no specific religious needs. That is, a child has physical needs, emotional and intellectual needs, he needs security and he needs standards of behaviour, but they are not religious in a narrow sense. Yet in a broader sense they are religious, since they are all expressions of a human being's desire to fulfil himself, and achieve his highest purposes, which for the Christian is 'to glorify God and enjoy him forever'. To impose upon a child something which is alien to his needs is quite contradictory to educational endeavour; to impose a Religion, with a capital R, which does not evoke any echo in the child's experience and which cannot satisfy his needs, is not only a wasted effort but may also destroy a child's true spiritual potential.

Emotionally, a child needs to be secure, and the roots of this need lie in the experience of love. A child therefore needs to feel that he belongs, first of all, to an intimate family, then to a community which cares for him. The aim, therefore, of Christian education is to build up a confidence in life and in people from the earliest years. This is done by persons reacting upon each other, and we know that Christian parents and Christian teachers and clergy, who really express this love and help the young to feel that they belong, are those who have the most lasting influence upon them. The home, the church, the school, are all communities in which children must be made to feel secure, so that they learn to trust and eventually themselves learn to love.

This is probably more true of the adolescent, who passes through a crisis of trust in his personal development. We tend to be much less permissive of adolescents than of children—there is far more freedom in an infant school than in a secondary school—and our most natural tendency with young people seems to be to criticise and condemn. There are many deep-seated reasons for this, the principal one being our reluctance to let them grow up, beyond our control. But the need for young people to experiment with their lives, within the context of security, is a need any religious community, church or school, must satisfy. This has implications for the methods by which we try to teach religion to adolescents.

The greater freedom of growing up also focuses upon a need of the young to be someone of significance, to have a personal identity of his own, an area in which personal integrity, personal values and personal choice are exercised. Some religious communities have difficulties in building up the young in this positive manner, because of a negative and repressive obsession with guilt. Many a young person's self-confidence and sense of significance has been destroyed by a morbid sense of sin. There is a normal sense of guilt to be encouraged in all children, a warning function as pain is a warning to the physical body, but it must be used to build up rather than to break down personality.

The need for moral standards are in part emotional as well as intellectual. They are emotional in that most children wait to be told what to do, only slowly learning to act responsibly and to behave at a genuinely personal level. Children, as indeed all of us, want an authority upon which to lean and where behaviour is concerned this authority has to be more and more convincing an authority as children grow forward into their adolescence. Intellectually, it is a growing sensitivity to the needs of others and a rigorous search for values which are sound and defensible in the light of experience.

These emotional needs are largely satisfied through individuals, and through individuals in communities. The school is one such community and teachers, as powerful individuals within it, exercise their major influence upon their pupils more by what they are than by what they teach. In this sense many are religious teachers rather than teachers of religion. A staff, even those not committed to a religious allegiance, can create a community of trust, of belonging, of standards and of an acceptable authority and so contribute richly to their pupils' religious education. On the other hand, negative responses of suspicion, condemnation or rejection, of poor standards and little authority of a school staff will undermine much that is taught of religion in the classroom or assembly.

The intellectual needs of the young can be summed up in their increasing desire to make sense of their total experience and their search for a meaning in life. Christian teaching should aim at satisfying their desire to make sense of life, within the context of a divine creation. The Christian faith is a frame of reference through which everything can be experienced, related and interpreted. As such it has an outstanding contribution to make to the intellectual development of children.

Until recently it seemed to be implied that understanding was of minor importance in religious teaching. We now know better, since thinking of a demanding kind at a high level of insight is necessary. The old conditioning question, What does the Bible say? must give way to the more insightful demand, What does the Bible mean? For this reason critical thinking about the Bible and religious belief must be encouraged in the late junior years in preparation for the critical years of early to middle adolescence. As we have noted previously, if the fruits of critical research into the Bible are not shared from an early age, childish views of the Bible linger on too long and retard the religious thinking of adolescents.

A major contribution to the intellectual needs of our pupils is the bridging of the two worlds, religious and scientific, which are beginning to grow apart by the end of the junior school. If a unified frame of reference is seen in religion, children should be encouraged to relate all that they learn, in all subjects, to this assumption. In this way they see that religion is not something separate, alien and imposed upon life, and they begin to comprehend, however dimly at first, that religion must be identified with life itself. Much of this can be achieved by across-subject teaching in the junior school, which I shall outline in greater detail later.

In addition, allowance must be made for the gradual development of a sense of time, concepts of the nature of God, of his activities in the natural world, of divine love, justice and righteousness and many other related concepts. Premature concepts can only be misinterpreted or distorted by children and the content of religious education must be radically revised in ways I suggest in Part II of this volume.

THE PLACE OF THE BIBLE IN DEVELOPMENTAL
RELIGIOUS EDUCATION

I have called attention to both the wasteful effort of teaching the Bible too early and also the difficulties this makes for children of limited development. I would like to correct the widespread misconception that I advocate no Bible teaching before the age of twelve. I do suggest a drastic reduction of Bible material in syllabuses before this age, but the difference does not lie so much in the quantity of Bible material used as the way in which we use it.

What We Should Be Trying To Do

The Bible is the major source book of Christianity *for adults*. It is written by adults for adults and is plainly not a children's book. To help children become familiar with it too early is to invite boredom and confusion, and even the most enthusiastic religious educator would not wish for this result to occur. What we must try to do is to help children to encounter the experiences of which the Bible speaks at suitable stages of their development. This means a severe pruning of Bible content in the early years, for it is only later that an understanding and appreciation develops of what the Bible has to say.

A clear distinction must be made, therefore, between 'teaching the Bible' and 'teaching from the Bible'.[9] We have been too concerned to teach the Bible as such to children, so that the whole drama of man's search for God is unfolded before them. Because much of the Bible is historical narrative it has been taught in this way, so that the sheer mass of material so often defeats both teachers and pupils.

If we teach from the Bible we recognise the linguistic, the intellectual and the experiential limitations of children in coping with it, and we select material which is suitable. The criteria for our selection would not be quantity but children's needs and experiences. In the primary school we tend to impose a series of Bible stories such as 'The Life of Moses' or 'Stories Jesus heard as a Boy' which appear to the adult to have continuity of sequence and significance. For the primary child they may have none, and, although interested and excited by them, he finds them alien and confusing. If, however, life themes are couched initially in terms of the children's experiences, biblical material can then be used to illustrate them. The Bible stories, narratives, psalms and other materials then may take on significance and meaning because they are seen by the child in a life context. Life is not used to illustrate Bible truths, but the Bible is used to illustrate life's experience. This is not a verbal, but a very drastic and far-reaching. distinction.

I would like to quote a teacher's reaction to this idea.[10]

> At first I was worried by the use of the Bible in what seemed to be an haphazard manner—for instance, in a series of lessons built round the theme 'Getting ready for Christmas,' one might find oneself using material from the Old Testament in one lesson (gifts to the tabernacle) and the New Testament the next (gifts from the wise men) both bound up with material from life (the dramatised choosing, packing and presenting of gifts). Or, on the theme of 'Hands', verses from the Psalms used with stories of the touch of Jesus' hands, together with the enjoyment of the use of our own.... If one believes that the test of truth for a child is whether it is true in his experience, and that experience must provide the central theme, then this gives order and continuity. Further, this is valid teaching. It is not a case of thinking, 'Well, until a child is capable of getting down to it, this is what we must do.' It is rather a case of seeing this use of experience as a wonderful opportunity of helping children to see God in their own lives and their own lives illuminated by God.

The use of children's experience illustrated by Bible incidents is consistent with the Bible itself. For the Bible is a narrative of men's experiences in their varying relationships with God. When we teach we intend to convey the truth of which the Bible speaks. If then we use it alongside, instead of imposed upon, children's experience, both the Bible and personal experience are illuminated and gain significance. In the child's view the Bible's value is enhanced because it is no longer seen as an endless and boring book, but a mine of relevant experience which is 'true to life'. (What some teachers report after using life-themes in the way I suggest is their surprise that they use a wider variety of Bible material in this way than they do in the more conventional approach.) If this emphasis is fostered throughout the primary years, the young secondary pupil is prepared both emotionally and intellectually for the more sustained study of the Bible in sequence and chronology which awaits him.

Teaching from the Bible in this way, however, should not stop after the primary school but should continue into adolescence. Even when more mature thinking is possible, orderly bible-theme teaching may be in too much detail. Further, it is important that our pupils gain first of all a clear grasp of the New Testament ethos before they turn to a systematic examination of the Old Testament. It should be constantly reiterated that much in the Old Testament is both pre-Christian and sub-Christian.

How life-themes, children's experiences and a more child-centred use of the Bible may be applied, is explored and outlined in detail in the second part of this book.

PART TWO

The Content and Methods

of

Developmental Religious Education

6

Early Childhood

MY INTENTION in reviewing a programme of developmental religious education is to confine my observations to children of school age. Although I narrow my definition of 'early childhood' down to the school years roughly covered by infant schools (approximately five to seven years) much of what I write could well apply to children of nursery school or pre-school children.

Physically, five-year-olds have lost their rounded baby appearance and experience a new kind of physical maturity. All kinds of physical skills are being learned, and there are less physical accidents because physical co-ordination is improving. Cutting, pasting, handling, hammering and use of crayons or pencils develop co-ordination into the sixth and seventh years. Within the period of early childhood, the important skills of reading and writing are beginning to develop. Intellectually, it is a period of pre-operational thinking, when isolated facts and ideas are the basis of reasoning in most areas of of the child's experience. Some children will already be dissatisfied with this egocentric mode of thought and will have thrown bridges forward towards a more operational form of thinking. However, this is largely experimental and the children do perpetuate many errors in reasoning because they are impeded by pre-logical (in an adult sense) thought forms.

For this reason fantasy plays a very important role in intellectual development, as well as contributing to the child's emotional growth. Because children cannot always reason their way into a situation, especially where there are problems, they will feel or fantasise their way into it. This is why play is an important educational activity. It is not merely a letting off of steam but play makes a serious contribution towards children's discovery of knowledge.

Socially, pupils still in the period of early childhood retain their self-centredness and their companions are ruthlessly exploited. A great deal of play is parallel play, and children sometimes will take turns exploiting each other. This stage shows a considerable social maturing taking place, when the children gradually become aware of social pressures and the need to become less egocentric in behaviour. Friendships, in the form of mutually interdependent relationships, may begin to emerge among many seven-year-olds, but these are liable to collapse overnight. The physical proximity of other children is more the reason for having them as play or work companions, rather than the result of real social choice.

Children in early childhood have a curious hybrid morality based upon a mixture of what we could call prudential and authoritarian behaviour. In terms of prudence the child is experimentally learning to avoid what hurts him. Perhaps this is how he learns a more authoritarian morality, since the power of adults to enforce their standards is to be feared. But what is right or wrong is largely determined for the child by what mother, father or other adult figures of authority say. Teachers, however permissive they may be, share this authoritarian role with parents.

There are many differences between children of this age, but the differences are less obvious than they will be in the next stage of childhood. Nevertheless, children in early childhood have a refreshing individuality about their behaviour, simply because social conditioning may not have begun to result in too many inhibitions. It is this aspect of early childhood which adults find so charming.

RELIGIOUS CHARACTERISTICS

Most writers characterise early childhood in religious terms of a parental figure. As we have previously noted, parents are thought by their children to have divine-like qualities such as omniscience, omnipotence and omnipresence. Some children, unaware of the length and finite quality of human life, can endow their parents with eternal life, in a physical sense. In the growth of a child's ideas of God this parental misconception is of great importance, for he is beginning to discover during this period of development, if he hasn't done so before, that parents do not know everything, have not unlimited powers and certainly cannot see everything or even be everywhere. A parent may become ill or die or desert the home. An inevitable disillusionment occurs, either slowly or in a spectacular manner, and results in the child's first religious crisis.

Bovet has described this period in the following way. To overcome the problem of disillusionment with parents, 'the child moves from deifying his parents to parentalising the deity'. To children who cannot think their way into religious truth, this is an emotional process in which their hunger for a certainty of trust is a reflection of their need for an infallible authority. It is therefore no surprise in our society that God is happily acceptable to young children as a male fatherly figure, symbolising masculine strength.

Consequently ideas of God have a clear pattern of physical identity and human characteristics. Hearsay experience of heaven lead to confusion but the explanations are simply resolved in physical terms. Here are some descriptions of God by children in infant school. 'God is the man in the moon. He has a round head and he has bent ears. He lives in a round home.' 'I think God might live up in space but I don't know. I think he might clean up his house sometimes. I think he might eat something like bread and sausages when he is hungry.' 'God is in the sky and you can't see him. He flies around. Sometimes he stops behind a cloud to have something to eat. He goes down to land at night to see shepherds and to talk to them.' These are good illustrations of how the children blend together physical ideas and fantasised thought.[11]

Despite their obvious interest in religion there is no indication that they may think in any religious sense. It is all part of the fascinating world of adult behaviour, conversation and ideas which they cannot understand. This is why I have characterised early childhood as pre-religious. Because the child has few doubts he accepts almost everything he is told or exposed to at this stage. This must not be mistaken for a profound phase of spiritual wisdom and insight. It is rather the contrary, for by his helplessness, his intellectual dependence and the social pressures to which he is exposed, agnosticism is foreign to the child.

Misunderstandings abound even among older children in an infant school. Here is a child's written version of the Lord's prayer:

> Our fathe wich are in heaven hallowed be thy name. die king of come die will be done on earth as it is in heaven give us this day of daily breath and forgive us...

These literalisms and distortions are the result of verbally conditioned learning without insight.

When, however, children pray in their own language they are more natural and talk as if to a human being. There appears to be a natural sense of the numinous, the mysterious and awesome, nature of God as the child sees him. Prayers may be trivial and very much at the level of asking for Christmas presents, but the feeling about prayer is a very strong one. What is a positive asset at this stage in relation to prayer is a negative and distorting influence regarding the child's view of the Bible. It is conceived as a book of magical veneration, written by God or one powerful holy person (the vicar or Enid Blyton), and is therefore to be accepted at a literal level as entirely true. And this is evident not only of the Bible as a book, but also of the stories, myths, legends, parables and metaphors of the Bible which feature so prominently in the sections on early childhood recommended by agreed syllabuses.

For this reason, because literalism breeds confusion, and creates the necessity for a great deal of later unlearning and relearning, I am suggesting that the content of religious education should be drastically reviewed for this age group. The danger of feeding in so much intellectual data is even greater when we see the child's willingness to believe everything that he hears. He is naturally trusting and his good-natured dependence can so easily be exploited. How we can help this natural religiosity in ways which build up his religious development, rather than interfering with it and negating it, will be explored in the rest of this chapter. With intellectual difficulties creating so many problems we shall be turning to the feeling and fantasising ways of learning as more appropriate for this age group. The reader should examine the varied evidence accumulated in other publications and if he remains unconvinced about the validity of this general picture.[12]

BASIC NEEDS

The younger the child the greater his emotional needs. It is evident for most children at the beginning of their school careers, that these needs are closely bound up with the transition from home to the new and strange but exciting larger society of school.

Security

Many children find their first days at school exciting and challenging, but even the most confident child finds it a demanding, insecure period. The routines of school are different from those in the home and the physical fatigue alone of this adjustment is a major difficulty. In our present system the length of the school day is far too long for many in the Reception classes and the law about attendance should be interpreted much more flexibly for those children who find a full day too tiring.

Part of the problem of fatigue is, of course, due to the

stimulation and excitement which the child experiences in the first years of schooling. A major need is to encompass the child with routines easily learned and happily accepted, which limit the adjustments he has to make. Ideally, the atmosphere of a Reception class should resemble a large family in a home more than that of a school, with the teacher as a mother figure to help the child transpose his dependence. What is lacking for so many children in infant school is the presence of male teachers, where strength as well as warmth and love are needed. This is of some significance in terms of religious growth, in that children should have experiences of father figures with whom to identify.

Dependence upon Adults

Personal comfort and assurance in moments of stress is a basic, constant need to be satisfied and a sense of trust must be nurtured. To many children from small families, the larger groups within a classroom and the still larger groups on a playground can be a bewildering, if not a frightening experience. To be one child among many may be a completely new event, which requires radical re-adjustments. Teachers do not always recognise that whereas they teach classes or groups of children, from each child's point of view there is a personal, not a group, relationship with the teacher.

The quality of this personal relationship, not between equals, but between a powerful person and her dependent, is the very essence of good infant teaching. The needs of the children are unlimited, even after the first settling down period. Putting on shoes, fastening clothes, going to the toilets, giving out paints, using a crayon, are settings in which personal crises will be experienced and require dealing with. Many infant schools do have across-ages groups, or family groups, so that older children do help younger children and a mutual interdependence can be satisfied. But always the major figure is the class teacher and a dependent relationship with her is the real foundation for trust and happiness in the infant school. It is also the foundation for spiritual development.

Social needs

While most children in their third year of the infant school begin to encompass the idea of a school community, the younger ones can only conceive of community in terms of small groups. Like adults they can be inhibited by size and this is why in a combined infant-junior school the first three years should have school assembly separate from the older pupils. In addition to size, there is also the problem of talking in language and about experiences suitable for too wide an age range. The occasional coming together of all ages in a full range primary school helps the young child to experience the entire school community, but held too frequently such an experience can be bewildering and retard rather than help the child's social ease.

Children of this age also need help with standards of behaviour. A great deal of mischievous activity occurs as they gain in confidence, and soon this develops into an exploration of what limits the teacher will allow. Severity is not necessary; often a word from the teacher is enough. Indeed, severity which inhibits children at this age can prevent a great deal of moral and social experimentation which is necessary for the child's social growth. Arguments with companions, sharing materials or tools, occasional tantrums and other outbursts are important for the child to encounter as part of his maturing. It is the balance between permissiveness and the observance of certain limits, gently but firmly imposed, which most helps the infant school-child. Here again the role of the class teacher has real religious significance.

Play and Fantasy

The imaginative explorations of children are, as we have already noted, an important intellectual as well as an emotional expression. Children should be encouraged in such work and play since they 'think' their way through their experiences in this manner. They will soon enough come to the factual, concrete thinking of the junior years; meanwhile their capacity for looking at the world in a fantastic way provides a vital process of self-education. This is why artistic activities of dance and mime, drawing and painting, modelling with plasticine and making things, and even talking are important as ways of exploring new ideas.

Play and artistic pursuits help emotion and intellect to fuse together into first-hand knowledge. It is true that children in the years five to seven still accumulate a large number of inert ideas, but the more first-hand sensory experiences of the world a child at this stage can encounter the richer his future thinking is going to be. Intelligence, we know, is affected very strongly by this early stimulation. Children of this age are far from apathetic, being full of eagerness to learn and to explore.

Perhaps this is one major problem for religious teachers, that they find it difficult to concede that such a serious topic as religion can be approached playfully or the child encouraged to fantasise about God. Yet this is his natural method of thinking, of expressing himself and searching. As we shall see when we look at methods of religious education for this period of development, artistic and emotional ways of understanding their experience are perhaps the most effective methods in the realm of religion.

Physical needs

I am not concerned here with matters of physical health and hygiene but with the much more basic need of children at this time to develop confidence and enjoyment in physical movement. What we call security comes in part from physical confidence, the exhilaration or enjoyment experienced in movement, and the successful mastering of physical skills. Part of their problem of using freedom, within certain limits, allowed by good infant teachers, is the removing of physical fears. The foundations of courage, so often held up as models in Christian saints and heroes, may have its foundation in physical confidence. Do we overprotect even small children so that they are soon conditioned towards unadventurous activities? We do not know what the connection is between physical and intellectual adventure, but it is obvious that there is some strong link. Children should therefore have opportunity for physical adventuring: some schools have playground apparatus which is designed for this purpose. We need to see the relevance of this need for laying the foundations of Christian character, not just as an aid to physical maturity.

Enjoyment of life

These are not unclouded years, but young children do have a natural spontaneous gaiety which is refreshing in its simplicity. Here is what some six- and seven-year-olds wrote into *Our Book about Happiness*.

Toyes make me happy and boatse make me happy and painting makes me happy and cats makes me happy. Doges make me happy and writing make me happy and fighting and watching television makes me happy.

Walking down sunny laes makes me happy. Going to the seaside in my mothers car makes me happy seeing all the lovly birds makes me happy I like walking my dog in the Park makes me happy.

In these delightful entries in infant diaries we can see the great capacity of children to enjoy life. There is a sense in which the aim 'that they may have life, and may have it abundantly' is realisable at no other time in life more than it is in these early years. What part should all this play in religious education?

If religion is to be experienced as relevant for these children it must be vitally and demonstrably concerned with the basic needs we have outlined. The satisfaction of these needs, directly or indirectly, comes through individual teachers, the quality of relationships within the small community of the classroom and the larger community of the school, and through the climate and general spirit the child experiences. At this age influence rather than instruction is more appropriate to the religious development of the child.

METHODS TO BE USED AND THE CONTENT OF RELIGIOUS EDUCATION

I begin with the methods rather than the contents of religious education because what is to be taught will depend very much upon the ways in which we are prepared to teach. Indeed, it is important that the ways in which teachers of infants are accustomed to stimulate their children in other areas of learning should not differ significantly from the way religious education is mediated. Later in school life more direct teaching may be useful, but between five and seven years a limitation of formal teaching will help the child to build up relevant experiences through which later Christian understanding will be formed.

To pupils in early childhood, knowledge is not piecemeal and not parcelled out into an artificial division of subjects. The most valuable work of infant teachers is to stimulate them to inquire, explore and examine all aspects of the world about which they are so naturally curious. Spontaneous questions about people, events, things, problems and many other experiences form the basis of a great deal of educational activity. There is a place and a time for practice in formative skills, but even here these best arise from the spontaneous interests of children. Children basically only begin to read and write when they feel there is something they want to read and write about. Motivation is the key. Much remedial work is concerned with releasing and chanelling the desire to be literate, more than with other factors.

In religious education at this stage to begin by talking in 'religious language' is as inappropriate as using advanced mathematical symbols with children. There must first be accumulated many and varied experiences of life of which religious language speaks. If we examine what children wish to explore from their own natural questioning, we hold the key to how this indirect method of religious education can be used to satisfy children's basic needs in the infant school.

Under headings such as children's experiences of

adult authority, experience of other children, their experience of the natural world, life and death, organised religion and school worship, spontaneous comments and questions were recorded by a group of Berkshire infant teachers over a period of several months. Where adults were concerned, the children discussed their mothers, the headteacher, getting on with adults in general, and behaviour problems such as disobeying a teacher or mistakes children made, such as an episode when the toilets were flooded. Opportunities arose naturally to look into their relationships with adults and the problems of people being together and sharing a community.

Children's experiences with other children evoked more frequent comments and questions. This is not surprising, since problems of social adjustment loom very large at this stage. Five-year-olds were concerned with the behaviour of a destructive boy, accidents to a building project when bricks were knocked down, criticisms of paintings, an unhappy child rejected by the group, and the use of strange words such as 'monitor'.

Among six-year-olds there were many more social problems raised spontaneously, such as a boy's aggressive behaviour, scribbling on a wall, ripping some sellotape, a girl in hospital, accidentally hurting a friend, impoliteness, and many others. On the more positive side ideas on sharing, helpfulness and co-operation were explored. A similar but more varied pattern was observable with the seven-year-olds.

Questions about the natural world in the early stage of the infant school were confined to the growing of seeds, a ladybird brought by a boy or queries arising from class nature walks. But later in infant schools it is noticeable that spontaneous questions increased greatly in number and variety involving problems such as gravity: why don't we fall off the earth? how do birds fly? does smoke go up to God? how are we born? why does frost disappear?

Life and death questions spread fairly evenly throughout the infant school showing a constant questioning about illness and dying, getting older, accidents, dead pets, rabbits, hunting, Mummy having a baby, prayers for sick people, and such queries as does a dead lamb go to heaven? Here is demonstrated the growing awareness of children about the finiteness of life and the insecurity this awareness brings, with a limited consciousness that 'religion' has something to do with all this. Questions about organised religion also arise frequently in the early years, and such queries as the function of cemeteries, Sunday schools, churchgoing, different kinds of churches, christenings, Jesus in a stable, and confusions of the vicar with God are raised. And naturally, worship in school assembly often becomes a topic for discussion or the starting point for questions. Questions are raised about a new boy who cried in assembly, making our own prayers, hearing a lovely story, talking to Jesus and hymn practice.

Any or all of these questions, raised in news-time, round a nature table or in informal conversation could become the starting point for exploring the significance of the experience 'in greater depth'. Here is an entry from the diary of a teacher of five-year-olds:

> Tommy brought a dead bird to school, which frightened a few of the children, but started off a spate of questions about death. To my astonishment the class produced a bewildering list of experiences of dead

guinea pigs, rabbits, dogs, tortoises, aunts and uncles, grandparents, and a parent. A little boy knocked down by a car was also discussed. It was not a morbid discussion but a real searching for the meaning of it all. There were queries about graves, funeral services, vicars, Jesus receiving the dead into heaven and how long do we all live?

After news time I found several children in and around the Wendy House holding a service for a dead pet and I felt here was an opportunity to explore other experiences of a more hopeful kind. Easter was about a month away. We planted seeds and saw how an apple fell off a tree and went bad before the apple seed fell into the ground. The children painted pictures of living and dying. I told as simply as I could how Jesus died and was still alive. Wherever we could a short prayer of affirmation about God's love was said. By the time Easter came the theme of life and death could be seen all round the classrooms. I felt they really were looking at the Easter scene in their own terms.

There is another extract this time from the records of a teacher of seven-year-olds:

The children considered Religious Education only as Bible stories and they were not very keen on this lesson. I decided to approach R.E. in a different way. Some of the children were looking at the Nature-Interest table and several of them thought a peacock was beautiful. Other children joined in, saying what they thought was beautiful; so I took this up and we had a discussion about beautiful things made by God, and the children suggested things they would like to thank God for. I made a 'Thank you Book' for them to look at and then put it on the Nature Table.

It took them three lessons to finish drawings and writing, cutting up a book and sticking paper in.

Then we went on to how we can thank God, besides making pictures, and we talked about prayers and being good. Some wanted to make up their own prayers and others didn't know how to set about it. So we discussed the Lord's Prayer ... again we made a book, slightly neater than the first one, with their pictures and prayers.

These two teachers are beginning with the children's normal and natural experiences, rather than imposing adult concepts and ideas unnaturally. A great deal of systematic teaching has taken place but a syllabus here would have been fatal. For the ground to be covered, the questions to be followed up, the activities expressed and the worship that stems from it all, emerge within each individual group. Even a very general outline might be constricting. But it is obvious that some themes will tend to arise time and time again involving adults, other children, the natural world, life and death and many others. If teachers are alert to these possibilities a very effective programme can be covered with such events as the seasons, the Christian festivals and the arrival of new babies in the children's families.[13]

Such questions to be explored and themes to be looked at, from as many angles as possible, may involve the use of the Bible. But it should be used sparingly at this stage. As long as it is used lovingly and with enjoyment by the teacher this is enough. To put the Bible in the hands of a child in an infant school, apart from the reading problems involved, is to create difficulties. Far better are imaginative activities of writing, cutting out pictures and adapting them, mime, movement and dance and any ways in which the children can genuinely explore in fantasy the experience they have encountered. Sybil Marshall illustrates this well[14] when she suddenly realised the rich imagery of the Psalms. Soon her children were producing a pictorial psalm, with every phrase an imaginative painting by a child. 'Sometimes the children worried about the meaning. "He touches the hills and they smoke". "What does that mean? Hills don't smoke." "Do they? What about volcanoes?"'. Mrs. Marshall tells how interest in volcanoes was immediate and many other interesting points were developed. 'General knowledge was not the least of the by-products of studying a psalm in detail.'

The psalms, of course, provide wonderful concrete images but the child must be helped to fill these out in his own time and through his own experiences. This is the function of imaginative activity. When it is stimulated the child participates in his own religious education. He is then exploring his own life experience in depth and is seeking to understand its meaning. Whether or not the words 'God' or 'Jesus' are being used constantly is less important than the assumptions of the teacher and the quality of relationship within the classroom.

What are these assumptions? They may be revealed as the opportunity occurs, but teachers will surround the children with a feeling of wonder in creation, the love which binds us together, the greatness of God, who is the Creator and Giver of all things, and Jesus, the strong kindly Son of God. Many of these ideas may confuse the children intellectually, but they provide a framework of meaning and cosmic security which they need at this stage. It is important that these assumptions should be felt emotionally rather than known intellectually. Much 'religious' material used with young children may only reinforce crude ideas if they are taught intellectually. If, however, they are explored by the child in artistic activities at a feeling level, the ideas and images can remain fluid, and mature as he develops. Activities such as movement to music and painting leisurely may help them to think more creatively, and less literally and verbally about religious experience.

WORSHIP AS RELIGIOUS EDUCATION

Children in infant schools have a natural sense of the mysterious and are very responsive to a mood. Perhaps for this reason our most effective religious education at this age is mediated through worship, when it is expressed in children's experience and language, and linked visibly with their basic needs. The danger, however, is that adult forms and expressions of worship will be used. There is an exciting and rewarding field open to those teachers who attempt to re-think worship through the eyes and experiences of their children.

Spontaneous worship in the classroom, often only momentary but having immediate significance, evoked perhaps by a glimpse of beauty at the nature table, can be a moving event if it occurs naturally. A child may wish to say a prayer, a thank-you to God or a sharing of some enjoyable event. To make children feel that worship must be confined to some set time and place is to negate the whole spirit of worship as an offering and a sharing. Where the teacher has an attitude of reverence for the wonderful and mysterious world of nature, of enjoyment of simple pleasures, of appreciating the work of others, of her own dependence upon God, then there is a worshipful atmosphere in her classroom which affects the children. With such a teacher, spontaneous worship will arise quite naturally and the children will respond to the opportunities presented.

For other teachers, however, whose attitudes are not so permissive or who are basically uncertain of their faith, such spontaneous worship may be an embarrassment or an insincerity. But something of the same worshipful and reverent attitudes will still be possible as general learning takes place. In early childhood these attitudes are just as important as the act of worship, formalised in the children's prayers, or other expressions of worship which may follow.

School assembly is perhaps too formal a term to describe infant school worship. Nine o'clock each morning is not always the most appropriate time for young children, who need to feel at home in smaller class groups and to share some experiences together, before they come together as a larger community. But whatever time of day the school worship occurs, it should be brief, colourful, beautiful, enjoyable, intimate and related to the direct experience of the children. The language used should be concrete and non-theological, couched in terms of the immediacy of infant schoolchildren.

Here is how one headteacher describes her own assembly.

We don't regard the assembly as a 'religious' gathering at all. It is a coming together as a family, of a group of people who are associated together, who are friends together, who have things that they want to share, things that they want to do and say. There may be music, any sort of music, from classical to pop, depending on the situation. Sometimes we have quietness. We sit down and it's a coming together at the beginning of the day, a welcoming of children into a community that means something, and a sort of sharing of experiences. This may mean entering into a discussion of what has happened to some of the children. Sometimes it is a news assembly, sometimes a birthday assembly. Sometimes we have something we want to talk about to the whole group. It may be something we've noticed on the way to school, or something the headteacher has been talking about. We may have extended an idea, music or a story. It's not 'religion', it's a coming together of a family.

Or again:

Spontaneity should run through all infant work. If a child brings to me something, as a child yesterday brought a Welsh hat, we look at this thing together. In our school this is for all of us. It's communion, if you like, but has no specifically religious backing. I believe this is a stumbling block because if you put in 'religion' it is artificial.[11]

Some teachers would feel that a more 'religious' form of assembly would not be artificial, and that all the sharing of such an assembly should be consciously and overtly directed to the person of God. Again, there will be great differences from one school to another. What one headteacher would find artificial another might not. But the heart of the matter is that worship for the young child must be at a personal, immediate level of experience if it is to be real. And it is more important that the qualities of love and caring, communion and sharing, be experienced in the worshipping community, than that the right 'religious' vocabulary be used.

The spontaneity of an infant school assembly may be seen in a large news-time, a sharing of interest, or an offering of some activity to God. Music and movement can sometimes be used in the sense that children can dance before the Lord, sharing their enjoyment. When children dance out 'Our Happiness', 'Our Home', 'The Sunrise' even 'Our Fears', it can be done spontaneously or it can be rehearsed a little beforehand.

It is optimistic to have children of this age participate as much as possible in their own expressions of worship? Here is a prayer by a six-year-old:

> Thank you for the sun that shines and food we eat and the snow that falls and the rain that falls and the flowers that grows thank you for the birds that sings thank you for the books we look at Amen.

And another six-year-old

> Dear Lord Jesus, We thank you for the Lovely things that you give us the dresses and our mouths and our hands and our fingers too Amen.

Some schools compile a large number of their children's prayers and make them up into a school prayer book. Over a few years a large selection is then available to be used in assembly.

Inevitably, the themes of the Christian year will arise in infant school assembly, especially the great festivals of Christmas, Easter, Whitsuntide and Harvest. The theological meaning of these festivals can be very confusing for children, or they see trivialities as all important. Here is a six-year-old's version of Easter:

> One day Jesus went to the sea of Galilee and saw
> Peter his disciple and said go and fech the other
> disiples and peter went to fech the other disiples Jesus
> said to them and said I am going to die on the cross
> and we will call it easter because I died on the cross
> and we will have easter eggs.

The profound meaning of the redemptive nature of the
cross, or the fact of the Incarnation celebrated at
Christmas time, cannot be grasped by five- to seven-year-
olds. How the festivals should be celebrated in infant
schools is always a problem to teachers sensitive to the
needs of their children.

How can these special and important occasions be
linked with the child's real experiences?

Christmas should be thought of in terms of homes,
families, the arrival of new babies, birthdays and other
happenings familiar to the child. A change from the
telling of the Nativity myths and legends and the
Nativity play, which children in primary schools become rather bored with, is to celebrate Christmas as a
birthday of Jesus, as a growing boy aged five, six or
seven years. How would Mary and Jesus celebrate such
a birthday? What kind of party would they have?
What kind of presents might the family give him? It is
interesting to see how to some children the thought of
Jesus as a six-year-old is a new and exciting idea. Some-
how, they feel, he suddenly grew from a baby in a stable
into a fully-grown man. Within such an imaginative
setting some of the stories from the first Christmas
might be told, but the emphasis will be upon the rejoicing and the importance of birthdays so that it will
be more real to the children. They will know a number
of carols. Why cannot children be encouraged to make

up carols of their own? I have seen a group of children too young to write, making carols by dictating into a tape-recorder. The whole emphasis should be upon the thanksgiving for a good and great man; an emotional experience, rather than any intellectual understanding of the Incarnation.

Easter. Young children should not be exposed, for obvious reasons, to the painful, horrific and often morbid details of the Crucifixion, although they cannot be protected from knowledge of these events. As with other festivals the emphasis in school should be emotional rather than intellectual, and it is the Resurrection with its hope, joy and new life which should be the emotional focus. Just as Christmas and normal childhood is the link with the true experience of children, so at Easter, the season of spring, the bulbs coming to life after the winter, and the new buds on the trees are the meaningful links with children's experiences. Their spontaneous questions on life and death, and the themes which arise naturally from these queries can be ways of leading up to the festival. In worship, Jesus as the new life, the light of the world, and other images may be useful. Again, it is more valuable to convey an attitude of joy and wonder at the event of Easter than to inculcate any ideas of salvation which are far beyond the child.

Pentecost is again a difficult concept for young children and the biblical narrative creates some terribly misleading imagery for concrete-minded children. Whit or white walks are still commonplace in the north of England, and some explaining of why white dresses are worn and new beginnings, may take place in such areas. In seasonal terms again, Whitsuntide coincides with the beginning of summer in our British climate, and the visible new beginning for the earth may be used. But a new beginning for the Church will be misunderstood by children, because their concepts of the Church are still crudely physical and limited.

Harvest is a festival which offers no real problems at this age for it is a gay, colourful and meaningful event, expressed so naturally by young children. Some critics would say this, of course, is not specifically a Christian festival. Nevertheless, if children can bring their gifts, not only the conventional fruit and vegetables, but also 'Things we enjoy and are grateful for', it has an important spiritual impact on the children.

I make no pretence of the fact that worship used in this matter is more difficult and more demanding of the infant teacher. It is, however, worship which most nearly meets the needs of children and as such requires no further justification. Teachers who use this approach find in it a rewarding and sometimes exhilarating experience for themselves, for they see the spontaneous response of their children in eagerness and simplicity as they share with God their daily life.

GROWING FORWARD

By the end of the infant school most children are beginning to talk and think in more specific Christian language, although they have barely moved from a pre-operational to a concrete operational mode of thinking. They are entering a pre-Christian stage in which much of their thinking may roughly approximate to the primitive materialistic religion of the early Hebrews. For this reason they need to relate their haphazard ideas together in some kind of pattern. Religion seen previously intermittently must now be explored more thoroughly, and we must look forward to children exploring more varied experiences of the world, of which religion and the Christian faith particularly is an important part. A great deal of preparatory work is still necessary before, in later years, any systematic study of the Bible can be anticipated.

As early childhood is left behind, children retain their enthusiasms and still believe without question much of what they learn. Wise teachers will not unduly exploit this eagerness at a religious level, but will begin to throw bridges forward to more discerning, less materialistic, beliefs which will endure through the later years of more critical attitudes. In this way middle childhood is seen in the next chapter as a vital sequence in religious development.

7

Middle Childhood

THE EARLY YEARS in the junior school can roughly be called the years of middle childhood, and while some characteristics still remain from early childhood in the infant school there are some important changes occurring in the development of the children. Physically, there has been continued growth into sturdy proportions, and greater co-ordination of the parts of the body make more complex skills possible. Children who have moved up from the infant school are often subdued at first, but their natural exuberance and vigorous physical activities soon become evident. Intellectually, most children will have achieved a level of concrete operational thinking in some areas of their experience; they are growing more and more able to relate facts together, to generalise and classify their experiences and to reverse their thinking processes. Emotionally, there is more control, fewer tantrums and a growing awareness of other people. Still egocentric in his thought and social behaviour, the child at this time is learning the art of personal relationships by experiments in friendships, often painful, but now on a more sensitive basis than previously. Mutual needs and reciprocity in relationships are still only vaguely recognised. Morally, the early junior is an authoritarian, content to accept the ruling of adults about what is right and wrong, the authority of parents giving way frequently to the authority of teachers. Morality is to be seen at this stage in a gradual recognition of the 'rules of the game', the recognition of objective laws which should not be violated even in play.

Obviously, within these general trends, children differ considerably from each other. In language, in skills in the basic school subjects, physically, emotionally and socially there are wide variations. Indeed these wide variations are becoming more marked during this period.

RELIGIOUS CHARACTERISTICS

The parental image of the deity is still strong and most children at this time see God as a human figure, with some of the physical limitations of a human being. His childish animisms, reflected in how he thinks of the sun and the moon, and his belief in fairies, goblins, Father Christmas and other mythical creatures are slowly receding before the pressures of reality. A literal belief in angels, as real people having physical substance and real wings, continues long after belief in fairies have been lost, possibly because they are associated with the authority of adults, the Bible and the religious language to which children are exposed.

The containing influence at this time is the child's concretistic thinking. His move towards a more realistic view of experience means that his religious ideas take on a materialistic and physical expression. He is reinforced in this by the language of religion, especially that of the Bible, since he takes the descriptive and metaphorical words at their face value and interprets them in a strongly literal manner. God therefore is still a large man, clothed in Palestinian garments, with a physical voice and presence, living in the sky but making visits to earth in person. He was about on earth much more in Bible times than he is now.

Fairy-tale characteristics are evident in God's magical powers, and although children use the words 'He is our father' and 'God loves us', these appear to be verbalisms often acquired superficially. God is still seen as a touchy, unpredictable, powerful and angry adult, often vindictive and harsh in his treatment of naughty people. At other times he is kind and loving, but always to be feared, rather like a mediaeval Merlin. His justice is strongly authoritarian, his edicts largely prohibitions, and vengeance appears to be one of the deity's major concerns. In all this the religious ideas of early juniors do seem to resemble strongly those of early Mosaic religion. Jesus and God are frequently confused, the names often being used interchangeably. Jesus has no clear identity and he takes on something of the magical aura of God. He features a great deal in prayers and worship, but there is little realistic grasp of Jesus as a real man.

On a level with his ideas of God and Jesus are the early juniors' views on the Bible, a magical and holy book ('magic' and 'holy' are usually synonyms in the child's language), written or authorised by God, totally true because of its divine authorship. This is a primitive literal and concretistic way of regarding the Scriptures. It would seem to be premature to teach the true nature of the Bible, since the concepts of multiple authorship, shades of truth, and the distinctions between myth, legend, interpretations of history, allegory and poetic expression are too abstract and subtle for children of this age.

Not surprisingly, with limited social experience and still unrealistic moral judgments, early juniors have no real insight into the nature of evil. Their own naughtiness is recognised, but this has no connection with thieves and murderers, who are really bad people. The devil is the black antithesis to God and only concerned, apparently, with spectacular evil. Prayers are growing in number and variety, and most children actually pray or desire to pray. Their prayers reflect a lingering egocentricity and materialistic desires. Even where other people are prayed for it is to make them more useful to the child, a consistent reflection of their social immaturities. But praying satisfies them and they find in it a pleasurable and happy experience.

We have written enough to indicate the quality of the child's religious life during this period. It is a time when a strong sense of the divine is interpreted in ways limited by the child's experiences of the world of human adults, the materialistic world he knows and explores, and lingering images of fairy-tale religion. Much of it seems artificial and imposed from outside the child but some of it is an expression of his basic needs.

BASIC NEEDS

What has the Christian faith expressed in the life of a school to offer children of this age, which will satisfy their basic needs?

Security

The need to be loved continues, especially as the

child's world becomes larger, more frightening, more demanding, and more complex. Parents and teachers can provide much of the assurance needed at this time. But since these adults, seen previously in divine and powerful terms, become reduced in stature, the need for some assurance beyond them seems to be deeply felt. A cosmic security, an ultimate faith in the kindliness of the universe, is not transmitted by verbal assurances, but by adults who themselves trust life, whether or not this is verbalised into a belief in God. Adults who demonstrate their belief in cosmic goodness, and who express this belief with warmth, devoid of embarrassment, in Christian terms, will doubly answer the needs of children. It is the demonstration of trust rather than the verbalisation which is the essential. To say 'My authority as an adult is based upon my conviction that God exists and is the authority for all I do' is obviously too abstract. But an adult who provides a framework of order for the child, who deals with him consistently, sometimes as a disciplinarian but always warmly, who worships and thus demonstrates his dependence upon God, is one who meets most effectively this need for security.

Community

Children still use their homes and family life as their base, but they need, as they grow up into a larger school, a feeling that the school community is one where they can be secure. Good relationships, happy experiences, enjoyable learning, all answer their needs, for alongside their need to be safe is their need to experiment and grow as individuals. The community of the school, by enriching social experience and by encouraging a child's exploring mind, provides a social and visible context for a maturing that the home alone cannot give. It is very evident that for many children, even at this age, the experience of a church will be unknown to them. This may be true whether they attend church or Sunday school or not, in that a religious community may not sufficiently demonstrate its care or concern for its children. The school then has a pastoral duty which extends far beyond the school itself in its concern for its children. This should not be a cosy protective society, but one in which misunderstandings are experienced and resolved, where problems of living and learning are faced and where growing up is an exhilarating challenge. Enjoyment of life is perhaps the hallmark of a good junior school community. This enjoyment should be expressed most effectively in the religious assembly which brings the whole community together.

Standards

Early juniors are becoming increasingly aware of the need to observe standards which are acceptable to adults. Their morality is essentially authoritarian and they seek for predictable patterns of behaviour. If these are not evident, they will frequently ask for them to be imposed by teachers or parents, in the form of rules to be obeyed. These rules should be clearly an expression of the school's concern for the protection and greater freedom of all its members. When children break the rules, vindictive punishment does not answer their needs; a recompense, or putting right of what was done, is more appropriate. Some insights, however limited, into the reasons for the rules should be offered to aid moral growth. To involve religion as an authority for these rules is an unnecessary and often cruel imposition, since a child's guilt at the violation of a rule may become intensified. How ridiculous to make a child feel he has violated God's commands by making a noise in the corridor. The way in which a school treats its rule breakers, repressively or educationally, is a test not only of its value as an educational society but also of its worth as a religious community. For one of the moral tasks of a school at this age is to moderate the natural vindictive tendency of young juniors towards a more sensitive understanding of the wrongdoers.

Meaning

Life at this stage is still very much a series of unrelated experiences, the child naturally and eagerly beginning to acquire all kinds of knowledge, information and skill without any apparent need to find an intellectual pattern. Later, in early adolescence, there appears a conscious search for meaning, partly because of external pressures and partly due to the maturing of the intellect, which then makes this search possible. At a more concrete and limited level the young junior needs to relate his many diverse experiences together. If he is in a good junior school, subjects will not be separated artificially on the timetable, but they will be related in projects and unified activity. The child explores the many and varied aspects of his world without labelling them geography, history, nature-study or English, and this approach helps him to relate life together. Yet strangely, the world of religion stands apart, as though it does not belong to this real world he is busily exploring. Instead of providing a unifying idea for all of life, it is separate and divisive, set too often in the strange context of an unknown culture of long ago. Stories about this alien-land and its people are enjoyable but puzzling, exciting but confusing, and their separateness is emphasised by an association with a special day called 'Sunday', special buildings called 'churches' and special settings called 'worship'. The need here is for the meaning of all that a child learns at this stage to be unified in God, and gathered up in the assumption, spoken and unspoken, that this is God's world, everything is his creation, and in him we live, learn, move and have our being. This assumption may be achieved by teaching life-themes, rather than 'straight' religion, but it will be most powerfully expressed in school assembly.

Fantasy and Imagination

The need of the child at this stage to unify the experiences, to relate them to what he can know and understand is limited by intellectual immaturity. It is natural that where his intellect cannot cope he will resort, as in early childhood, to earlier ways of understanding, namely through fantasy. This is the activity of imagination, which later develops into a more disciplined poetic or artistic expression of experience. Fantasising is still a natural mode of exploration for early juniors, for where they cannot think their way into an experience, they can at least feel their way into it. Perhaps we need to encourage more and more of this imaginative probing at the feeling level to balance the prosaic concrete-mindedness of children at this stage; it is the gateway out of the concrete prison of literalism into a wider spiritual world. Younger children are naturally creative and imaginative. Too soon self-consciousness appears, the factual 'real' world intervenes, and some children never seem to look at life with the eyes of imagination again. The need is there, often unanswered, and religion, far from stimulating the imagination, may only stifle it by trying to impart a body of historical information.

Although I have stressed, especially with younger children, that the most effective religious education is through influence, by the quality of personal and group relationships and the climate of understanding and tolerance within a community, the time of middle childhood is a period when some planned content of religious teaching is possible. The children are ready to explore through their experiences, and to interpret them, in planned and systematic lessons.

We have already noted, and demonstrated elsewhere with a great deal of evidence, that Bible teaching is an inadequate content for religious teaching, since it asks too much from the child and does not involve enough of his experience to make it relevant or sensible. Much more consistent with the intellectual and emotional needs of children at this stage is teaching by means of themes, based upon the real life experiences of the children. I have called this teaching by life-themes. Life-themes relate religion to life by emphasising the total unity of experience. They demonstrate the inter-relatedness of all knowledge, and across-subject teaching is employed so that religion is not confined to a separate role on the timetable. Where the Bible is used, it should be used not in a systematically historical manner, but where it is relevant and can illuminate and enlighten the child's knowledge. In this way the child's experience and the truths of which Bible narrative speaks interact upon each other, enriching both.

A life-theme can take any area of a child's life, of which he has first-hand knowledge. It should be about matters in which he has a natural interest and in which a large amount of diverse detail can be explored, related together into a meaningful unity and seen at a level of religious thinking within the capacities of the child. Examples of life-themes possible for first year juniors are:

Homes.	Feet.
Friends.	Clothes.
People who help us.	Breakfast time.
Pets.	Seeds.
Shepherds and sheep.	Birthdays and Parties.
Hands.	

Examples of life-themes possible for second year juniors are:

Holidays.	Milk.
Journeys.	Fire.
The seasons.	Gifts.
Bread.	Beginnings and endings.

Any of these themes may have 'religious' and biblical illustration throughout; they may begin with a religious emphasis or end with religion as a focal point.

This is not, of course, a final list of possible themes. Once we begin to look at the first-hand experiences of children many other themes arise naturally, sometimes from stray questions of children ('How is sand made?' leading to a theme on the seashore), sometimes from topical events (A Royal Wedding leading to themes on Marriage, The Home, the Birth of Children) and sometimes planned with the calendar in mind (St. George's Day leading to a theme on Helpfulness).

Nor do I suggest that the themes outlined above need be confined to the year I have stated. Some teachers may see possibilities for a younger or older age group. It is important, however, to make sure that themes are not repeated in the same school with differing age groups lest children become bored with over-familiar material. There are many themes possible, and the more imaginative the teacher the more themes and their elaboration will occur to them, so that the danger of repetition is remote. Teachers experienced in this approach also soon discover that one life-theme may lead quite naturally to another, and the problem then will be how to control the flow of ideas rather than how to stimulate them.

For those who are uncertain or unconvinced let me outline in detail how the content of life-themes could be used. I shall illustrate at length from two of the life-themes for seven- and eight-years-olds, 'Shepherds and Sheep' and 'The Importance of Bread' in the 'Readiness for Religion' series.[15]

Sheep are known to young children through first-hand experience of travelling through the country-side, or through television programmes, films, books, nursery rhymes and many other sources. Even so, knowledge of sheep within the cultural setting of the child, unless he lives in the country-side, is very limited. To expect children to understand, even in an emotional sense, the rich metaphors of the Bible about sheep and their shepherds is to ask too much. Consequently, we have devised a life-theme based upon what children already know, helping them to explore it from the inside—what it feels like to be a sheep—then developing these feelings and ideas across to Palestine and the various ways a shepherd cares for his sheep. Although Jesus said 'Feed my sheep', not 'Fleece my sheep', some real understanding of the true value of sheep and the relationship between sheep and shepherds can be built up. This preliminary exploration is not wasted, but helps the child to see the 'real' experience underlying the religious language he will hear later. The intention of this theme is to get the child to identify emotionally with sheep, to understand their dependence and so to feel his way into the religious metaphors rather than intellectually understand them.

The theme explores, through a series of work cards, various experiences the child has encountered and supplies new ones, always with the town child in mind. The following are suggested:

> Finding out about a sheep farm.
> Dipping and shearing.
> Wool and its uses.
> Shepherds and sheepdogs.
> Shepherds in Palestine.
> Sheep in Palestine.
> A sheep's day: Morning.
> A sheep's day: Evening.
> Feasts and festivals.
> Models and music.
> The Good Shepherd.

Each card can be shared but may also be used by individual children. A great deal of searching, enquiring, thinking, creating sounds, situations and music, and many other activities are devised to stimulate the children. The various experiences can be woven into themes for worship, for festivals and other school events. The theme could last a few weeks or an entire term, depending upon how much of the timetable a teacher will want to use. Biblical material plays an important part but arises naturally out of the treatment of the theme.

Similarly, with perhaps slightly older children, we have explored 'The Importance of Bread'. They see bread, they eat it, but most children these days have little insight into its real nature or its significance for daily life. Again, there are many rich religious meta- phors which are lost, simply because experience is limited and children need to explore in depth what experience of bread they already have, if they are to recognise its centrality and to apprehend its religious significance. By making bread, seeing its elements, watching yeast working, and discovering for themselves the mysterious process of breadmaking, we are putting real life experience alongside religious truth, so that knowing ordinary life at depth becomes a religious experience.

Again, a great deal of our theme here is directed to emotional and physical knowledge of bread, as much as intellectual understanding. Here are the work-card headings:

> The food we like and the food we need.
> What goes into bread?
> Flour from wheat.
> Growing the wheat.
> The wonder of yeast.
> Making our own bread.
> Making bread in Jesus' home.
> A modern bakery.
> Bread for the world.
> Special occasions.

The emphasis is upon children doing things, finding out, experimenting, thinking creatively and getting in-

side their experiences. Artistic activities are constantly
suggested. The Bible is used to illustrate the theme and
the religious metaphors are introduced where they can
be relevant and illuminating.

All the other themes listed can be developed and
elaborated in similar ways. Although children's work-
cards, such as those we have devised in our series, are
useful, these themes can be implemented by using
material normally available in the school and classroom. To take one example, the life-theme of 'Home'.
We could explore with the children their experiences in
the following ways:

1. *Our own homes*
   The house we live in.
   The furniture we use.
   How we keep warm in winter.
   How we keep cool in summer.
   The family—what we do together; picnics, play, look-
      ing at TV, going to Church.
   How we help each other in the home.

   Things to do:
   Describing in words, drawings, painting models, dis-
      cussion: playing at being fathers and mothers; keep-
      ing a 'House Diary'; Finding out songs, poems and
      music about homes. Making up prayers for the
      family, poems about our homes, etc.

2. *Homes in Other Lands*
In very cold countries
   Why homes are different to ours. How they are the
      same.
In very warm countries
   Differences to and similarities with our houses.

The home of Jesus
His house and his family.
The furniture.
How they kept warm.
How they kept cool.
What the family did together.
How they helped each other.

Things to do:
A classroom frieze or exhibition of what we find out; magazine cut-outs; models, paintings; what we saw on television programmes; stories about homes in other lands; some stories of Jesus' home; Make-up some stories, songs, poems about Jesus and his home.

3. *Families on the Move*
Have you ever moved house?
Nomads, Gypsies, Fairground and Barge children.
Refugees without homes.
Homeless in our country.
How people help them.
How we can help them.

Things to do:
Descriptive activities about homeless people—pictures, stories, etc: raise a school collection; give a school concert in aid of homeless people; collect clothes from home.

4. *Plan a festival of 'Home'*
The theme for a week's assembly led by the class. If this theme is chosen for November and December, the festival can lead naturally to the celebration of Christmas—'Welcoming a new child of the Family to the Home'.

Some criticism will be voiced that there is not much 'religion' in this kind of theme. If by 'religion' is meant the introduction of Bible narrative, prayers, hymns, mention of churches, Christ, God and other terms, these can be used in abundance in the context of the child's experiences. The home of Jesus can be explored, not in abstract or impersonal times, but through the eyes of the children and in comparison with their own homes. A great deal of factual information about Palestine can be learned in this theme, preparing them for later Bible study. References to Jesus' childhood are few in the Bible, but there is a great amount of material about the Palestinian home embedded in the stories, parables and teaching of Jesus. There are a large number of pictorial background books for the Bible, suitable for young juniors, which can be consulted. The Bible stories and their meanings will not be understood, but the factual descriptions can be used, to underpin the child's idea that here was a real society, of real people, in a different climate, in homes different in many ways from our own, but in other ways rather similar.

The religious significance of this theme is, of course, much deeper than the use of 'religious' material. The nature of the home as a place of mutual help is explored, the physical environment is only the setting for the love which binds a home together, and a concern for those who need our help, as well as a thanksgiving for homes in a final festival of worship, are all religious in a broader and a deeper sense. Under 'Families on the Move' the question, 'Have you ever moved house?', with the fears, misgivings and insecurity children often feel, will arise naturally, and the experiences of homeless people can be understood at an emotional level.

There will, almost inevitably, be children from broken and unhappy homes in the classes, as well as one or two from a local authority children's home. We must be sensitive to the distress such exploration may cause these children, but we should also be aware of the therapeutic value of dealing with such a topic for children deprived of normal home life. We are here, in the setting of love in a school, going beyond fallible parents to the eternal ever-loving and caring God. If we cannot help children to explore their insecurities, and cannot help more fortunate children to be sensitive to the needs of other children, our teaching must remain at a very superficial and unreligious level.

METHODS TO BE USED

With all ages, it is essential to involve the pupil as personally as possible in what he learns. The most effective learning occurs when children do not passively receive what is given to them but are actively engaged in the learning process. A failing of so much religious education at all levels of development is that much of it has tended to be teaching of an instructional kind which has not sufficiently engaged the pupils in active personal search. When we consider that religion is essentially a personal quest, it is surprising that heuristic methods used in other subjects taught have not readily been used in religious education. This in part stems from the misconception that we are solely engaged in handing on a body of truth, but, of course, in order to be a 'truth' it must be recognised as truthful in the experience and convictions of the child. This is why education as a personal encounter is at the heart a basic method of religious education.

The use of experiential data in life-themes will

personally involve children in what they learn and create active interest in understanding what is taught at a deeper level. But a change in content is no guarantee that children will be more involved. The themes we suggest and the specific material outlined will be still-born if they are 'taught' in a formal sense. The themes are meant to be actively explored, so that children at this age will know, either at first-hand or by reflecting upon their past experience, what is the meaning or significance of it in a broader spiritual setting of Christian belief.

Let us take the theme of 'Bread' as an example. It would be very simple to 'teach' about bread, telling children stories about bread, with pictures and actual ingredients such as flour or yeast, showing them how bread is made. Seeing the teacher mix the ingredients and even make bread is one step better than being told about it, but even this is no substitute for the children making bread themselves. The feel of it, the labour of it, the exciting action of the yeast, the heat of the oven, the concern to bake to the right texture, are all important for a child to 'know', in a society where his bread is rarely baked at home but only in a remote mechanised bakery. The real and the symbolic imagery of bread, so frequently used in the Bible, cannot be fully understood without this prior experience.

The 'Readiness for Religion' series is designed deliberately to help the children explore and experience as much for themselves as possible. This is why the 'Things to Do' are not tacked on at the end to satisfy educational conformity. They are an integral part of the material, to be used alongside the text, not only after it. Sometimes children will read the material on their own, sometimes in groups, sometimes looking up new facts, discussing the suggestions, preparing their diaries or mounting an exhibition display. Sometimes the teacher will talk to the whole class, sometimes to a group, sometimes to an individual child. There will be some teaching, with different numbers of children. But the major amount of time will be helping the child to search and discover, stimulating him to look in more detail and find out for himself, and to record and share his findings in some way with the rest of the class.

For this reason teachers should always bear in mind from the beginning how the children may wish to present the material as a climax. Sometimes an exhibition, either in the classroom or in the hall, might be suitable so that the whole school can share what has been done. At other times personal diaries, class workbooks, or a wall frieze will be enough. For our purpose, perhaps the most effective way would be to gather up all that has been done in worship. This could be a spontaneous class worship or a carefully planned school assembly in which thanksgiving, rejoicing and sharing of, for example, 'Homes', can be the theme. The theme could be for a single assembly or for a longer period.

The material for young juniors, in our series, namely 'Shepherds' and 'Bread', are meant to be used flexibly and are certainly not designed to be followed slavishly. Teachers will find some of the ideas for children's activities possible in most classrooms, with only slender resources and equipment available. But where there are particular difficulties in a situation it is obvious that the content or direction of a theme will have to be changed. The adaptation should not, however, be made at the expense of children's explorations, for to do this would be to destroy the whole intention of the series.

I clearly recognise that both the methods and the contents I have suggested for young juniors are more difficult than more formal methods involving straightforward telling of Bible stories. More effective means of education are always more demanding of teachers, yet few teachers worthy of their calling would say that easiness should be the criteria for what they teach and their methods of teaching. The criteria should be what is desirable, what is possible in terms of pupils' abilities, and what is practical in the classroom. It is desirable that children should participate as much as possible in their religious education. What is suggested is consistent with their experience and within the limits of their abilities. The themes and methods set out in this chapter have been tried in normal classrooms by teachers with no special training and found to have been practical. All teachers involved state that this new approach is most demanding but they also report a greater sense of enjoyment and participation by children, and so a more satisfying and rewarding experience for themselves as teachers.

A few teachers do have reservations and are somewhat uneasy that the results of teaching life-themes are not very tangible. When one has told a Bible story, the results seem to be much more clear-cut, because one has been dealing with material officially recognised as religious. The evidence, however, indicates that these so-called tangible results are not so tangible as they appear. They only appear to be so in the teacher's mind. We have all been taught by rather systematic bible-learning methods, and it is natural that we should feel some insecurity when we leave them and enter into unfamiliar territory. We may reflect, however, that what is unfamiliar to us is not unfamiliar to the child and our primary concern is to provide him with what best meet his spiritual needs.

Worship is, or should be, an emotional as well as an intellectual experience. It is the lifting of the heart to God, and for children it should be a sharing of their life experience with him. Too often the language of worship and the experience of which it speaks is far too adult for children of this age to gain from it anything but a very solemn feeling that here is something special and different from the rest of their experience. While I would wish to retain a feeling of reverence in worship and a sense that here is something of great importance, this should not be an excuse for superficial piety, nor should it absolve us from the need to make worship an experience related to the real life of the child.

A great deal of worship may arise, as with children in the infant school, quite spontaneously in a classroom situation, around the nature table or at some quiet moment of wonder. 'Thank you God, for the icicles', Alice exclaims, as she watches them hang outside the classroom window, and she quite naturally sits down and writes a poem which others in the class may want to share. This simple incident happened, without false piety, during a life-theme on 'The Seasons'. A similar spontaneous incident occurred during news-time, in a period when 'People without Homes' was being discussed, and a desire was expressed to 'remember people without houses of their own'. Here was a wish, which the immediacy of the eight-year-old needed fulfilling at once. Not every teacher may feel that this spontaneous worship is possible. And it is not desirable that pietistic teachers should pop up with prayers on every occasion. But what occurs happily for both children and teachers can serve to introduce children to the naturalness of prayer.

For the daily school assembly itself, themes related to real life experiences should predominate. Although the spontaneous worship, which arises naturally in a small group, is not possible in a larger assembly, as much spontaneity as is practical should be retained. We cannot make children worship by imposing an adult form of worship upon them. For this reason worship which is a genuine expression of children's lives will be shared by the children much more than adult hymns, prayers and readings. Some adult expressions are unavoidable, and sometimes desirable, as in singing some of the great hymns of the faith. Children may not understand what they mean but may get some glimpse of their power and purpose in the singing of them. Glimpses, however, are not enough and adult forms should certainly not be the regular diet for junior worship.

Life-themes on which several classes are working may form suitable materials for assembly worship. It is essential that children themselves present their own findings, or produce a dramatisation, or talk about their exhibition of work. Young children, while poor readers, can often talk quite fluently and intelligently to other children, especially if there is a tradition of this kind of assembly in a school. Pupils who would be tense at taking a straight Bible reading may happily and naturally talk about the theme they have worked on over the last month or two.

Topical events may also be used as worship themes; not events, of course, which only adults think are striking, but events known by the children and interesting to juniors. International events, for example, which involve conflicts of a political nature, may be very topical for adults but not for children. But the launching of a space satellite, a royal journey, a visit to the town of children from another country, a television programme, sudden weather changes, school events, are all part and parcel of the real world of children.

Recurring themes for worship are seen in the changing calendar, especially the great Christian festivals of Christmas, Easter and Whitsuntide. Harvest festivals in schools are always enjoyable, although some theological purists would deplore their pagan origins. Some of our suggested life-themes could well start or have their climax in the Christian festivals and form a week or more of worship themes. For example:

Christmas—Homes; Gifts; Birthdays.
Easter—Shepherds and their Sheep; Beginnings and Endings.
Whitsun—Fire; Journeys.
Harvest—Bread; Breakfast time.

In this way some of the intellectual difficulties of festival doctrines involving profound theological truths may be minimised for children, because they are connected with experiences they are exploring. The crucifixion, for example, with all the complex forces of evil and hatred involved in it, will be theologically beyond this age level, but as a celebration of a shepherd giving his life for the sheep it is more comprehensible. The profound truths of the Incarnation will not be perceived at Christmastime by young juniors, but some of the sentimentality of the festival can be countered by looking more deeply into their own homes, by exploring imaginatively what the first 'home' of Jesus was like and in what kind of home he celebrated his birthday. In the past, imaginative teachers have tried to make the Christian festivals alive in this way, but it has too frequently been haphazard and couched in language and experience far too adult.

Participation by the children and their teachers as a regular and normal procedure, should be more than announcing hymns or taking a reading. The material itself could well be written by children. I know of a junior school, where the pupils have over the years written their own hymns, written their own prayer book and used their own poems, stories and dramas. These are some of the prayers:

Eight years old
> Thank you God for making us do our work and please help us to help the teachers do their work. Please make the school a happy place.

Nine years old
> Dear Father,
> Our lives are very jolly but please help the people who have not got such good homes, food or clothes as us. Please help me to make their lives as joyous as ours. We thank you for our trees our flowers and everything else in this world today. Amen.

Here is a hymn written by a pupil using a well-known tune with different verses for differing seasons:

Content and Methods

Autumn has riches
  Brown, gold and silver.
Diamond bright cobwebs
  Hang on the boughs.
Crystal clear dew-drops
  Found in the morning
God made all these things
  Just for us all.

Springtime awaits us
  Sunshine is clearer.
Shoots will be peeping
  Through the cold ground.
Birds will be singing
  Grass will be green and
Little blue violets
  Soon will be found.[16]

Some primary schools with a musical tradition write words and compose their own hymn tunes. In these schools assembly is often a joyous occasion for a junior orchestra to lead worship by making a joyful noise unto the Lord.

Here is a prayer, spoken by a backward seven-year-old reader into a tape recorder and used in assembly.

I think you are wonderful,
Making the sunrise and all that.
You are big and I am small
But you are not too big to love us.

Is not this a valid prayer of adoration?

Underlying all that I have written about worship for this age is that children have very little rational under-

standing of what worship is, but they have an un-
sophisticated sense of the numinous, a natural awe by
which they can feel their way into worshipping God.
Linked with this is their spontaneous expression of joy
and a happy willingness to express themselves, given the
encouragement and the freedom. Mysteries were en-
tered into by primitive peoples in the past by mime and
dance, sometimes a ritualised and sometimes a spontaneous offer of worship. Why cannot these be used by
younger children, trained and encouraged to feel their
way into what is so difficult intellectually? Mime and
dance do help a child to fantasise and develop imaginative insights perhaps otherwise unexplained.

Some eight- and nine-year-olds in a Norfolk primary
school[17] took part in an experiment on these lines.
They covered a wide range of intelligence, were under
an experienced teacher who was interested in Dance,
but who had no special training or qualifications in
Dance Method. Music was provided by a record player,
supplemented by a tape recorder. The subject chosen
was 'Creation'. After discussion it was decided to use a
version of the story by Heinz Kuhne[18] designed for
children with a reading age of eight years. Considerable
time was spent in listening to gramophone records in
order to select suitable music. An outline of possible
movements was then worked out; experimentally building up the dance occupied two periods of thirty minutes
each over several weeks.

The final form was presented to the school as a
narrative with music, mime and dance to illustrate the
theme of 'Creation'. Here is an extract from this
presentation which took fifteen minutes:

NARRATIVE	MUSIC	MIME AND DANCE
'In the beginning God created heaven and earth, and nothing grew or lived, and it was quite dark.'	Electronic music.	Children lying. They move at will (chaos) getting up and down, moving at any speed in any direction. All lie down again at end of music.
'And God said, Let there be light.'	Planet Suite. Gustav Holst (Uranus—first few bars only).	All move in unison signifying order as God shapes the Universe. Stand up in four jerky stages, make a circle, raise hands and eyes to Light above centre...

This was a fairly polished, well-presented performance, but other themes and other groups have danced and mimed more spontaneously. Young juniors have presented two or three minute mimes, to suitable music, of 'Happiness', 'Sunrise', 'Fear', 'Home' to the delight of other children in assembly, as an offering to God. Both the spontaneous and rehearsal presentations will help children to stretch themselves imaginatively in their approach to worship.

In brief, worship for early juniors, and much of this is valid for the junior school generally, should engage both the interest and activity of the children, so that by participating in it and providing as much of the material as possible themselves, theirs shall be a genuine offering to God, a joyful giving and sharing of their own lives and their own school experiences.

The time of worship at the very beginning of the school day is not always the best time for young children, as we have already noted when discussing worship in the infant school. The immediacy of experience and its natural expression in worship may require a warming up period in school. Mid-morning, end of morning or end of day assembly would help, for then children will have some immediate common experience to share with each other and with God.

GROWING FORWARD

By the time most children move into the second part of their junior school course a number of developments in thinking, literary skills, social experience and other areas have taken place. Teachers of young juniors should be aware of these later needs and capacities for which their work is a preparation. In religious education this is vital because continuity of religious development is necessary if children are to grow forward into a more mature apprehension of religious truth.

The evidence indicates that the final years in the junior school are vital years for the formation of attitudes, for developing a sensible and less primitive way of looking at the Bible and as a preparation for the thoroughgoing critical reassessment of values which takes place in adolescence. Late juniors are beginning to resemble pre-adolescents more than children. These and other important changes will engage our attention in the next chapter.

8

Late Childhood and Pre-Adolescence

I HAVE GROUPED TOGETHER the last two years in junior school and approximately the first two years of secondary schooling under this one heading, because there are many characteristics similar to both groups. In the first stage of secondary schooling the pupils do seem to resemble their junior school counterparts more than their older fellow pupils in the same school. In physical terms, late childhood and pre-adolescence appear to be almost identical as, on average, early pubertal development is occurring. As the age of the onset of puberty comes earlier, so childhood seems to become foreshortened for large numbers of our children. Physical maturing is accompanied by an interest in 'pop' singers and teenage ideas, even by nine- and ten-year-olds, a feature of development which still seems to surprise many adults. This development is particularly evident among girls, the boys being on average much slower developers. It is noticeable that the body is already beginning to prepare for puberty, and indeed it is reported by the evidence of many headteachers that more girls in junior schools than in previous times have began to menstruate by the time they leave.

Intellectually, they retain the characteristics of childhood, thinking still at a very concrete level, able to classify and relate factual material together with in-

creasing skill. This is possible because of a greater
facility in reading, writing and use of vocabulary, and a
considerable desire to accumulate a great amount of
factual data. Many late juniors and early secondary
school pupils delight in collecting objects. It is a peak
period for collecting stamps, pictures, pebbles, coins,
autographs and many other things. The pupil's
approach to knowledge is not unlike this accumulation
of objects, the amassing in detail of facts to be stored or
related to each other.

Emotionally, this tends to be a settled period of stability in which the stresses of early childhood have now
disappeared and the ferment of adolescence has not yet
been encountered. At the beginning of this period there
is still the refreshing whole-hearted enthusiasms, un-
touched by later self-consciousness and guarded cynicism. Socially and morally at this stage the peer group
begins to exercise greater influence. For most children
reciprocal relationships are now established and mutual
social obligations are recognised. What the peer group
regards as right and wrong now tends to dominate
choices of all kinds, from dress to morals. This dominance of the majority in judgment can be seen in the
eleven-year-old who said it was obvious that the world
was round. When asked why he was so sure, he said,
'Well, we voted on it and everyone said so.' In its own
way, this is still an authoritarian morality, exchanging
the authority of the adult world for that of the group.

Towards the end of this period, by twelve to thirteen
years of age, this facile assurance is breaking down, as a
much more critical approach to thinking develops.
With brighter pupils more abstract relational thought
becomes possible and a dissatisfaction is felt with con-

crete ideas. For many in their pre-adolescence the image of 'the teenager' is attractive, so that what we might call 'teenage values' are already exercising a real influence.

Individual differences are growing much more in evidence and it is obvious that while many remain children physically, intellectually, emotionally and socially, others are far ahead in one or more of these areas by the age of twelve. The generalisations I have made are only meant as rough indicators of general development.

RELIGIOUS CHARACTERISTICS

Religious fantasy is now left far behind, although certain fantastic religious ideas still linger on. Cruder anthropomorphic ideas of God are giving way to a supernatural rather than a superhuman view of the deity. Limiting physical ideas still persist in some concepts, such as God speaking with a physical voice, the concrete elements of communication still dominating the pupil's ideas. From about ten years onwards, and more with increasing age and experience, there is a great deal of intellectual confusion as the child tries to adjust himself to a more realistic theology. It becomes clear, for example, that children begin to recognise the problem of God being everywhere and at one place at one particular time. To overcome this problem God must be conceived of as a spirit, not bound by physical limitations, but the child's natural concrete form of thinking makes this concept difficult for him to grasp. These concrete limitations do not seem to begin to disappear in religious thinking until about thirteen years of age. Thirteen, on average, appears to be the decisive age for most children, when they move forward into more adult thinking about religion.

At this in-between stage a dualistic view of life, and especially of the natural world, is beginning to manifest itself. God, magic, long ago, are beginning to be seen in contrast to the absence of God, natural law and modern living, and while they are not yet seen in opposition to each other there seems to be little relation between these two separated worlds. The accumulated evidence of this dualism is marked from the mental age of ten onwards and is perhaps one of the sources of the confusion in religious thinking I noted earlier.

Another source of the confusion seems to be a thorough misunderstanding of the nature of the Bible and its inspiration at this age. The Bible is revered because it is an ancient book, appealed to by teachers and because of its content. Any stories about God or Jesus cannot be thought of as false or inaccurate to the late junior. It is still an authority in a literal verbal sense, although its multiple authorship is now being recognised. 'It is true because it is in the Bible' still persists well into the secondary school, although a few minor mistakes may be allowed 'due to the writing down'. More pupils at this later stage also are seeking to relate Bible incidents to the present, and feel that the God of the Bible should still be active, but what I have called 'an isolation-in-time concept' still lingers on.

In contrast to this, indicating the compartments in which many children think, God is thought of as geographically distant 'in heaven'. The figure of a man is now giving way to symbols of power and glory. Prayers to God increasingly become more altruistic, as the pupil becomes socially more sensitive, and concerned with self-examination of his own inadequacies.

Prayers to be a better person, set prayers, and petition for protection from danger are at their peak, as the pupils become more aware of life's pressures and physical suffering becomes more real. Even so, this is a period of semi-magical praying, seen in the reasons the child gives for prayers coming true.

Guilt is felt in relation to specific and concrete actions, not as a general condition, and for the junior, God is still more interested in vengeance than in love. The early secondary pupil shares this cruder idea, but is obviously dissatisfied and is on the borderline of recognising that divine love and justice are compatible. Bad people, for example, are not seen as an undifferentiated whole and his group condemnations are beginning to be qualified. His view of evil is still very unrealistic, but he views the devil very much as he has changed his view of God, moving towards a more supernatural idea. The devil is now not so much a man as *the* evil spirit and master-mind behind the spectacular evil deeds of evil men. As yet this has little connection with the pupil's feelings of guilt.

Late juniors and pre-adolescents see the boyhood of Jesus more realistically, regarding him as a normal boy with the normal mischievous activities, but there were no really grave misdemeanours since he would be rather serious-minded. When it comes to the manhood of Jesus, he is seen more as a master-magician and emphasis upon miracle is common until about thirteen years of age. There is very little insight into the mission of Jesus, his Messiahship and the relevance of his message. These limitations appear to reflect the natural limitations of understanding both the human situation and inter-personal needs generally.

Emotionally, there is still a very strong identification with belief in God, largely authoritarian in nature. But some confusions and doubts are already evident, even though they do not become frequently vocal until the end of the second year of secondary schooling.

BASIC NEEDS

Again, we must ask what are the basic needs of pupils at this stage of development and how the Christian faith, taught and expressed in a school community, can help to satisfy these needs?

Security

While, in one way, this is a period of increased assurance, a growing awareness of the insecurity of life is seen in prayers for protection, for recovery from illness and later for help in personal problems. Although peer pressures replace a great deal of adult authority, later juniors and pre-adolescents still require the guidance of adults who are positive and assured about life. A trust in teachers is a common experience in the smaller, more friendly and intimate atmosphere of junior schools, but our present system leaves a lot to be desired when an eleven- to twelve-year-old transfers to the larger and therefore more impersonal life of the secondary school. The majority of pupils, in areas not organised on comprehensive lines, do carry a sense of educational failure from their junior school for not having gained entrance to a grammar school. However good relationships have been until this point, there is an inevitable sense of devaluation which both junior and secondary schools should be aware of in spiritual terms. Teachers in both kinds of schools should indicate by their attitudes that the children are valued in their own right, irrespective of their promise or attainments as school pupils. Teachers, who on the whole are the successful products of grammar schools, may find it difficult not to devalue less able pupils, but for Christian teachers to betray this superficial type of segregated thinking is a demonstrable contradiction of what they are trying to teach.

Community

Late juniors and pre-adolescents are very sociable, indicating a strong need to be supported by their immediate peers and by the larger community. Their groupings at this period tend to be single sex groupings. Firm friendships based upon mutual inter-dependence are very marked. There is sometimes a curious tendency in some junior schools to treat older pupils, especially boys, less warmly and more sternly than younger pupils Although they are growing up, the warm personal interest of friendly adults is needed, even though some greater restraints may have to be exercised. This greater discipline is very evident to pupils as they move into the larger, more impersonal, atmosphere of a secondary school. There is much to be said for transfer to secondary education at twelve or thirteen years of age, so that there is a move into a genuinely adolescent community. Certainly, large secondary schools should be so organised that a smaller community than the whole school can be the secure link of each pupil with the larger community. Apart from difference in size, there is also the change from class teachers to subject teachers, and the close friendly relationship known before with one trusted adult is no longer possible.

The pastoral concern of subject teachers, whatever

their subject, needs to be more visible and conscious in the first years of a pupil's secondary school career. Form teachers should be responsible for doing more than calling a register and personal links should be formed and strengthened with individual pupils. We have not accepted the American pattern of a counsellor in our secondary schools; we should be training and equipping teachers to see this as part of their spiritual as well as their educational responsibility.

Again, the focal point of community is the morning assembly, in which the work of the whole school, its concern for all its members, and an expression of enjoyment of being together, can be shown.

Standards

Late juniors and pre-adolescents require rules which make for good relationships in running a community. It is interesting to note that as pupils get older more rules appear to be necessary, and more repressive measures may be used when they are wilfully disobeyed. Vindictive punishment is, of course, quite contrary to the spirit of religion. How the community of a school treats its offenders is, as at other ages, a test of its claim to be a religious community, and, as with younger children, the emphasis should still be on putting things right. More insights are now possible into the reasons behind certain rules, and the moral appeal seems naturally to be at the level of mutual convenience. The golden rule of 'do unto others as you wish them to do to you' needs no overt religious sanction behind it, for it is such evident common-sense to pupils at this stage of their social development.

Again it is the spirit rather than the letter of the law by which any school educates its pupils. It is how staff members themselves are considerate of each other and of their pupils, how fair in their dealings with everyone in a class, and how the teacher controls himself, which is the greatest help to the young. For at this stage, teachers are popular who are seen to be consistently just and concerned with individuals. And popular teachers are more likely to be imitated and their teachings believed in than unpopular teachers.

Meaning

The search for meaning is now at the start of a new intensive phase, for the onset of clearer thought creates problems in the child's religious ideas. Childish concepts are clung to, but the doubts and confusions are already appearing. At previous stages the child happily kept together unrelated and often contradictory ideas, but now he is becoming aware of the need to relate and reconcile these apparent contradictions. We require an intensive effort in teaching religion at this stage to help him grow a 'one-world' view of life, rather than a dualistic system which separates religion from the rest of life. There is the further task of weaning him away from his 'isolation-in-time' ideas where religion is concerned. And while he still retains a positive belief in God, we should anticipate his next stage of critical thinking by encouraging him to think critically about religion, God, and the Bible within the context of belief. We can be sure that if he does not do this within the context of belief, he will do it later in the context of unbelief and doubt. There will be some who will protest that this would disturb the innocent faith of the young too soon. The evidence, however, is that this disturbance is already beginning to operate from ten years on, and that we have waited too long in preparing children for their natural and necessary doubts.

Exploration

Although the search for meaning can now be engaged upon in more realistic terms rather than by fantasy and play, imaginative thinking must not be driven out by an exclusively rational approach. In all this our pupils need to explore at both levels, in terms of fact and in terms of the poetic, for the language of religion is the language of fact, embedded in a historical faith. It is also the language of poetry, set in parable, allegory and metaphor. Even when the language of the Bible is in prose, its profoundest meaning can only be understood in poetic terms. How we can train our pupils to speak and to understand in both languages is one of the major tasks of religious education.

THE CONTENT OF TEACHING

To answer the intellectual needs of pupils in this period, approximately nine to twelve or thirteen years, two differing emphases of teaching seem to be appropriate. One is the continuance of life-themes, discussed at length in chapter seven, but at a higher intellectual level to meet their widening powers and interests. The other is the beginning of the more familiar pattern of Bible-centred material, but simplified and placed in a more meaningful sequence to overcome the limitations of language, ability and experience elaborated in Chapter 3. The two differing emphases could be used alongside each other, as I suggest from the last year of junior school, but teachers may feel one type would be more suitable for their pupils than the other. It is important, however, to recognise that the way in which they are to be used should be consistent with the total pattern of religious development. I shall outline each emphasis in turn and then discuss how they may be used together.

Life-Themes

The rapid acquisition of facts and the eagerness of junior school children to learn on a broad front of experience, reveal their need to relate all that they learn to a significant pattern. Religion can supply this pattern not by being placed alongside what is learnt, as a separate subject, but as a series of ideas and experiences interwoven into all that is known by the child. Children at this stage see knowledge as a unity. What they learn is not automatically broken down into subjects such as English, history, geography, arithmetic, art and religious knowledge. These are purely artificial divisions of knowledge to be learned and experience to be encountered. This is why across-subject teaching is becoming more common in junior schools and subject divisions, although necessary in certain skills such as arithmetic, are not as rigidly followed as before.

The unifying principle, spoken by the teacher or to be assumed by the children, is that all we learn about the world is a knowledge of God's world, of his creation and his power. This could be scornfully dismissed as nebulous pantheism, unless rooted in a concept of the creative power of the Christian God, whose nature and love are demonstrated in Jesus Christ. But long before this can be perceived intellectually, children must have the foundations laid so that they can understand later that God is, in Paul Tillich's phrase, 'the groundwork of all reality', and is to be sought not in the strange and exotic, but in what we know of his world.

Here then are some life-themes for the last two years
of the junior school which can be taken within the
specific periods designated as 'Religious Knowledge' on
the timetable, or treated as across-subject themes. The
second alternative is to be preferred as a constant re-
minder to both teacher and pupils that religion and life
are one. Those teachers with a more subject divided
timetable may within the traditional 'religious' periods
still use life-themes. If they are not spread into other
periods these themes will obviously take much longer to
complete. The suggestions listed are meant to be implemented as flexibly as possible by individual teachers
according to the possibilities allowed by the timetable
and the needs of the children concerned. Some suggestions of possible life-themes are:

> Myself
> Creation
> Light
> Water
> Sound
> Growth
> Air
> Law and Order
> Names
> Stories

Many other themes are possible, and indeed, one could
take most of the themes suggested in the last chapter
for younger children, and plan material for an older
level. These themes here, however, do seem more
appropriate for nine- to eleven-year-olds, and also for
less able pupils at the beginning of secondary schooling.

The 'Readiness for Religion' series presents examples
of how these life-themes can be used for religious teach-

ing. These are 'About Myself', 'Light' and 'Symbols' (involving names and stories). It will be worthwhile to discuss these three themes in a little detail.

Nine-year-olds are still egocentric enough to be thinking about themselves a great deal of the time, not simply emotionally in the natural self-centredness of young children, but in a lively curiosity about their bodies, their growing powers and everything which affects them intimately. Some might complain that a theme directed to the self will only reinforce childish self-centredness. But where it is used to lead to a clearer perception of oneself, a wider view of experience, an awareness that what happens to me happens to other children, and a clearer sense of whàt a human being is, a theme of this kind can be deeply religious.

This is the aim of the theme 'About Myself'.[19] Children are encouraged to keep a workbook, or a diary, entitled *How I came to be* or something similar. Five booklets are available for children to work on, stimulating them to find out as much as possible about themselves. The five booklets are titled *What I am Like*, *What I can Do*, *What I know*, *What I find Wonderful* and *What I can Do with Others*. An examination of the first book alone reveals the wealth of teaching possible under such a theme. Starting with a physical description done by the children themselves, they are led to discover that every one of them is different, by such devices as seeing their fingerprints and comparing their names. This leads to the beginnings of things, how we are made, the beginnings of man seen through the legends, stories of people long ago and also in simple evolutionary terms. There is a wealth of biblical and other religious material woven into this theme.

The children see themselves in the great human tradition, and the Bible, early stories and the like are all related to what the child is now. In terms of subjects on the curriculum this involves English (writing and discussing), history (how ancient people thought of themselves), geography (invoking people of many countries), nature-study (the growth of the body) and many artistic activities (poetry-writing, painting, making things, music). Imaginative teachers will realise the opportunities presented by so many differing but related suggestions, and should prune or extend the ideas as is necessary.

This enrichment can be seen in the life-theme of 'Light', suggested for nine-year-olds, involving a great deal of scientific discovery. Here is an effort to relate what can be known about the properties of light, with the constant symbolic use of light in religious language. Here are the titles of the six booklets to be used by the children.[20]

1. *The Growth of Light*—man's discovery of various artificial lights. As light has come, so man has been less afraid. Jesus casts out fear.
2. *The Source of Light*—the sun. Without light there can be no life. Man first worshipped the sun, then the God who created the sun. The sun as the centre of our universe. Men use light for describing God and Jesus.
3. *The Image of Light*—we need light to see. How the eye works. Seeing things in different ways. Mental images. Jesus as the image of God.
4. *The Path of Light*—finding your way by day and night. Looking at the sky. Lights that guide and warn. Jesus gives guidance.
5. *The Power of Light*—light as a source of energy—

mechanical, chemical and electrical. People who em-
ploy this energy. The power of Jesus.
6. *The Wonder of Light*—light and colour. The artist's,
poet's and musician's use of light. How they have
been inspired by Jesus the Light.

It will be seen that a great deal of biblical material is
used, and an exciting merger of many fields to be explored is possible, within the unifying purpose of the
New Testament message.

We have recommended for the last year of junior
schools and also in early secondary schooling, as a
further preparation for the problems of dealing with
abstract religious ideas, a theme on 'Symbols'. The
world of children is full of symbols—words, maps,
traffic lights, signposts, advertisements—all of which
represent something real to them. All symbols have a
significance, often stemming from the past, and we have
selected four of these, common in the experience of
children, which have a religious significance within the
comprehension of pre-adolescents. These four symbols
are dealt with in separate books under the headings of
'Names, 'Numbers', 'Stories' and 'Actions'.[21]

To take 'Names' as an example, children are asked at
the beginning to compile a 'Name Dictionary' with
double columns, one dealing with Christian names and
their symbolic meaning, and one with surnames and
their symbolic meaning. In looking at how Christian
names arise, the significance of the baptismal service is
explored, and the meaning of many names are looked
at. Our indebtedness to many other people including
Greeks and Romans, Early English and Normans for
our names is examined, but especially the religious impact of the Jews and later through the Puritans and

Huguenots, the importance of the Bible is investigated by the pupils. Surnames, nicknames and fashions are all searched into and the religious theme of symbolic meaning is reiterated throughout.

The whole theme, taking in also Numbers, Stories, and Actions, is designed to do three things—to help pupils integrate many varied items of knowledge within a meaningful pattern of religious thought, to make them sensitive to the fact that life is full of symbolic meanings not noticed before, and that when religion speaks in symbolic language, it is not speaking in obscure or irrelevant terms, but in terms rich and significant.

Religious themes

Until this period pupils should not have been taught the Bible so much as *from* the Bible, where biblical material can illuminate the real experience of children. A total view of the Bible in terms of the development of religious ideas, the historical sequence of events in Old and New Testaments, is best left until pupils are well embarked upon their secondary school course. A great deal of teaching *from* the Bible will have occurred and a wide diversity of biblical material will have been used to illustrate experience up to this time. There are, however, two systematic bible-themes which, for want of a better term I call 'religious' themes, which could well be used alongside life-themes, from ten years onwards.

The first is some kind of introduction to what kind of book the Bible really is. Research indicates a great deal of confusion and misunderstanding in the child's mind on this, which often distort how later in secondary school he thinks of biblical truth. Before a pupil embarks upon a historical study of the Bible, within his comprehension from twelve to thirteen years onwards, it seems important for him to have some framework of meaning through which he can view the Bible and some clear concept about the nature of Bible truths. Otherwise, the pupil's confused thinking will continue far too long and contribute to his condemnation of Bible teaching as childish and irrelevant.

With this major problem in mind we designed a theme in the 'Readiness for Religion' series dealing with this intellectual need of pre-adolescents, consisting of a series of four books under the general heading of 'What is the Bible?'[22] The first book encourages the children to ask what books are for and to explore the different categories of books they use. Some, such as cookery books or knitting pattern books we expect to be completely accurate. It is their purpose to help people bake or make things and complete accuracy is part of their purpose. Fiction should be explored, the best of which may be untrue but still 'true to life'. Although these books are untrue they are still important for helping us to understand life. For example, Mark Twain's *Tom Sawyer* is a wonderful story: although Tom Sawyer never existed, he is probably a mixture of all the boys the author had ever known. Similarly history books, dictionaries, encyclopaedias, books on travel, adventure, sport and other topics can be shared, examined and placed into categories meaningful to the child. Against this background the Bible is then seen, both as a library containing all kinds of books and as having many different types of material. A valuable part of this first book is a section on newspapers, how reporters work and what reporting means. Some cross reference to the way in which the Gospels were written is featured alongside this.

The remaining three books explore the various contents of the Bible in more detail. One book considers some 'True' stories about real people such as the intensely human story of Philemon, and the diaries of Dr. Luke. Another book is concerned with helping pupils to look at myths, legends, interpretations of real events and allegories, some of which are 'untrue' or only partially true, in a historical sense. Examples of these are the creation stories, the great flood, the tower of Babel, some stories from the Exodus, one or two Davidic stories and the allegory of Jonah. All these can be placed alongside the kind of books ten- and eleven-year-olds are using, and compared. This is an age when the children are familiar with national myths, legends and allegories such as St. George, King Arthur and many others.

A final book on *What is the Bible?* deals with the poetic elements to be found in the Bible. This involves not a reading of the psalms or the songs of the Bible, but by stimulating the writing of children's poems, prayers and hymns, to help the children to have insight into parts of the Old Testament which served as the hymnary, liturgy and prayer book of the early Christian Church.

The total effect aimed at is to introduce children, at their own level of experience of literature, to the real nature of the Bible and to lay the foundations for their understanding of the true authority of the Scriptures. It anticipates that they need weaning from a literal reverence for the Bible towards a critical reverence, so that they may begin to see scripture as true in a spiritual and not necessarily literal sense at all. Earlier in this chapter I suggested that unless we help our pupils, at this stage in their search for meaning, to think critically but reverently within the context of belief, they will do it later in the context of unbelief. Some people find it incredulous that we should attempt to introduce ten- or eleven-year-olds to the higher criticism. In terms of their growing experience and ability it seems well within their capacity, if there is constant reference to the literature they know at first-hand for themselves.

The second 'religious' theme, to be used alongside the life-themes suggested from nine roughly to thirteen years of age, is the first systematic exploration of the significance of Jesus. If life-themes have been the major content of religious teaching up to nine years, then a considerable amount of material in which Jesus is central will have already been experienced. In such themes as Shepherds, Bread and Light what Jesus meant for the world is introduced in terms of experiences known to the children. And already children by the age of nine in attending church or Sunday school, in the celebration of Christian festivals during school assembly and by a great deal of incidental information gained from many sources, have some hazy and confused notions about the birth, childhood, teachings, death and resurrection of Christ.

Until this age, as we have seen, many of the teachings and certainly the mission of Jesus will not be grasped because of limitations of mental powers and restricted experiences. At this stage it would seem more appropriate to dwell upon Jesus as a strong, loving man, who went about doing good, than upon his teaching or his messianic mission. Late juniors still think of Jesus as some kind of master-magician, and his miracles tend to obscure the manner of man he was.

A straight reading of a Gospel, even that of St. Mark, is too confusing for children of this age, both because the content is difficult and the language is archaic as well as too adult. School Bibles, even shortened versions of various kinds, are not very appropriate either. A great number of Bible background books about the land and people of Palestine are very good as reference books, but they do not, after all, provide the foreground of Jesus himself. I would suggest that stories told by the teacher about 'What Jesus Did', mostly deeds of goodness, which are not directly related to miracles, but show his dealings with people, will build up this positive manly picture of Christ which late juniors can respect for the right reasons. The calling of some of the disciples, Jesus and the crowds, Jesus and the children, Zacchaeus, tests of endurance such as a mountain ascent and long journeys, Gethsemane and some of the stories of the Passion, should be used sparingly but alongside the life-themes suggested.

By ten years of age and in the early secondary school course this picture of Jesus should be widened and supplemented as our pupils become more aware of the personal issues of life which they are beginning to face. The teaching and source of the miraculous events featuring Jesus can be looked at more fully, provided, when the Bible is referred to, some accurate concepts of 'What the Bible Is' have been built up. A series of edited translations of the Gospels are soon to be available, with a controlled vocabulary for pupils of a reading age 9 to 12 in view. A series of five are planned and I recommend the first two as reference texts for use by

late juniors and early secondary school pupils.²³ Alongside the texts there are many suggestions of 'Things to
Do' for pupils, encouraging them to depict or reinterpret what they have read.

When we turn to the secondary school we can readily
see that duller pupils should still be working on life-
themes, similar in content and significance to that of
late junior children, but average to bright pupils may
begin a much more systematic study of parts of the
New Testament. Given the groundwork of thematic
teaching in primary schools most of this material
should be fresh and interesting to them. The teachings
of Jesus, for example, including the parables, now come
within their intellectual compass and they themselves
will be ready and willing to translate them into modern
terms if provoked to do so by stimulating teachers.

We are now in the familiar territory of Bible study
where some systematic teaching of a Bible-centred
character becomes more appropriate. Lest we resort
merely to teaching Bible-content and face our pupils
with a rather dull and irrelevant series of narratives, I
would make three suggestions which secondary school
teachers may find helpful.

First of all, leading pupils through the life and
teachings of Jesus does not exonerate us from the need
to link the New Testament with the present twentieth-
century world in which the pupils live. Although the
focus is upon Jesus, the question of how he is relevant to
the experience of the pupil still remains the important
issue. 'What does this teaching mean?' is not an abstract, but a concrete and personal question, 'What does
this teaching mean for *me*?' We may have to begin
with the relevant experience of an eleven- or twelve-year-

old, explore it in general terms, read and discuss the parable or teaching which should illuminate it, helping the pupils to build a bridge of meaning between the two. If we cannot find a relevant experience in the life of our twentieth century pupils, it is questionable whether this particular teaching from the New Testament should be taught at this stage.

The second suggestion concerning the more sustained Bible study possible with early secondary school pupils I would make is that none of it will make much sense until some basic understanding is achieved of what kind of book the Bible is and is not. Since we cannot assume that a theme of this kind has been explored in the junior school, a secondary school teacher should be alert to the need to spend perhaps a term on this. Since I have described how such a theme can be explored in junior terms, here is how a secondary modern school teacher is using it with his first and second forms.[24]

'What is the Bible?' From the beginning we can elucidate (from class answers) that it is a library, and the books in it can be counted. The division of the school, or public library, gives a basis for classifying the Bible library into fiction and non-fiction. The next step is to ask for subject classification into History, Law, Belles-Lettres, Religion and so on, but it will be quickly found by the pupils that there is seldom a clear-cut division in the Bible, and that the main distinction of this library is the unifying God-centredness of all the books. That this is a parable of life is not likely to escape class or teacher. The 'fiction element' of the Bible, lest it be dismissed as simply untrue, should be tackled firmly (*a*) by reading an extract from modern fiction, with true-to-life characterisation and drawing the parable (In what way is this episode true, although invented?) or (*b*) by selecting poetic phrases of obvious intention, but dubious or nonsensical literal meaning ('My true love hath my heart and I have his') or (*c*) by examining the real meaning of Santa Claus, for instance, and the driving power behind St. Nicholas (a knowledge of right personal relationships). From this and from the library analogy it is simple to move to such questions as: Where do we look for scientific facts? Is history true? How do we know it is? Is history science? What *is* science? What is science true about? —or any other similar scheme of advance to the stage 'How can we tell if something written is true or "just words"?' Can we examine the Bible in the same way? (We can, but children often say 'No'!) Why not? And examine the answers in the light of what has already been agreed, and show that it is vital to a logic-supporting faith, like Christianity, to be self-critical.

Mr. Simpson has many other interesting ideas, but discussion, he suggests, should lead to the further vital question, 'What is belief?' and by exploring their own and biblical experiences the pupils come to see a clear distinction between 'belief that' an event, a situation, a happening occurred, and 'belief in', a personal emotional response which is rarely demonstrable (as 'belief that' is demonstrable). Mr. Simpson further feels it valuable not to take a dogmatic party line, and asserts the method used is that of Our Lord himself—'You know the answer from your own experience. Think!'

The third suggestion about the use of Bible study in the first two years of secondary schooling is that we deliberately exclude a systematic study of the Old Testament. This is intentionally left until the next stage of religious development, not because a study of the Old Testament is unimportant, but because by leaving it until later it allows a concept of the New Testament ethos to form in the pupils' minds. Unless some firm ideas are formed of what Jesus means for the world and what is the message of the New Testament, much of the Old Testament may be taken on its face value. Instead, the New Testament must be used as a yardstick by which the value of the Old can be measured. The slaughter of the Amalekites is not consistent with the love of God seen in Jesus Christ. In this way, pupils can be introduced critically to the study of Old Testament religion. This is not a mere debunking exercise but an examination of the way men have searched for the truth, encountered God and misunderstood or only partially understood their encounter. Meanwhile, the basic need is to build up some understanding of the Jesus of the Gospels, the spread of Christianity in the ancient world, how the Gospel came to Britain, and to our own community. Once it is seen, however partially, what Christ means for the modern world, then is the time to go back in history beyond Christ's time, to see the answers man made. I shall look at the problem of Old Testament teaching in more detail in the next chapter.

METHODS TO BE USED

As our pupils increase in age the methods we use to educate them undergo subtle changes. The fact that as they become older their span of attention, their vocabulary and their grasp of more complex ideas improve, often convinces us that they can be taught more directly by being talked to or talked at for a large part of each schoolday. There is a place for direct teaching in the form of talks, stories and even lectures with pupils from nine to thirteen years, but the use of these traditional methods is now regarded in many subjects as of limited educational value. A revolution in teaching methods, which involve the personal activity of pupils, is slowly affecting our schools. Unfortunately, religious education appears to be a subject where traditional methods seem particularly well entrenched.

That our pupils *can* listen more intently and intelligently is no reason why the oral teaching of the teacher should dominate religious education. If we intend to teach religion as an authoritative body of truth there may be some educational support for 'instructing' in this way. But if we accept our aim as helping a child in his personal search for truth and religion, and truth can only really be acceptable if it is done through a personal exploration of experience, then the limitations of teacher-teaching methods will readily be seen.

The life-themes suggested for older juniors are designed, as with younger juniors, for a learning method more than for a teaching method. The teacher stimulates, guides, discusses, helps and occasionally, as the classroom situation or individuals demand, teaches. Sometimes, for even a few consecutive sessions, a set lesson may be followed, but the major activity must be with the pupils themselves. In the study of Light, for example, teachers could eliminate a great amount of personal experiment with the qualities, colours and nature of light, teaching 'the facts' to the class as a whole, and even verbally drawing attention to the analogy of Jesus as the Light of the World. To use the theme in this way would be to destroy its essential purpose. It is only by experiment, by thinking for themselves, by entering not only scientifically but poetically or musically into the experience of light, that the religious analogy will begin to be real.

The authoritarian teacher may feel much more satisfied that something definite is being taught when he is talking, but is this not merely changing the egocentricism of the child for the egocentricism of a teacher? As the Newsom report says, 'It can indeed produce the state of mind which one headmistress recently found among her girls. They believed the Bible to be true, but unimportant for them, though they recognised that it probably was important for people like her' (p 58).

The danger of an oral-teaching method dominating religious education is even greater in secondary schools, where sometimes teachers are strongly subject-minded and see that one of their main goals is the imparting of information. The activity approach of many junior schools is gradually permeating our secondary modern schools, especially where average to backward pupils are clearly not good information fodder. The evidence is unmistakable, however, that later in their school career adolescents voice a great deal of discontent, if not hostility, about authoritarian teaching, especially where religion is concerned.

All teaching, of course, need not be authoritarian and I readily concede that the years roughly from eleven to thirteen are good 'teaching' years, when pupils seem more willing to learn, eager to please and have better relationships with teachers than in later secondary schooling. Yet the utmost effort should be made, as with life-themes, to encourage the personal participation of pre-adolescents in their own religious education. Looking up their own material, translating stories into their own experiences, dramatising on a tape-recording or on the stage their own interpretations, painting, drawing, sculpting, creating models, stained-glass windows, diaries, newspaper reports, discussing anything which relevantly engages their own authentic experiences, is important in any subject. In religious education it is vital.

One criticism teachers often voice is that much less material is covered at the expense of more activity by the pupil. This is an accurate observation, although not, I think, a valid criticism. If we are concerned that the quality of a truth is understood, because the children see it is true to their own experiences, the time spent in activities which explore experience is a solid educational investment. As in all subjects, the balance has to be held between the quality and quantity of what we teach. In religion, especially in the pre-examination years, where a quantitative assimilation of material to convince examiners is not yet an important feature of school life, our major concern should be for quality of insight into religious truth achieved. Ultimately, teachers, as well as their pupils find this much more rewarding than the quantative aim of 'getting through the syllabus'.

WORSHIP FOR PRE-ADOLESCENTS

It is difficult to write generally about worship for this wide age-range of nine to approximately thirteen years, involving two differing types of school, junior and secondary. I shall therefore try to deal with them separately. Much of what I wrote for young juniors, in the previous chapter, applies to worship in the junior school generally, including older pupils. Older juniors are, in fact, much more confident and more able to participate in school assemblies than those in their first two years of school life. A junior school, where there is a happy tradition of participation by staff and pupils in morning assembly, will allow for a reverent expression of the older juniors' natural exuberance, a sharing with God of the pupils' enjoyment of life and also of his anxieties and fears. The older junior, however, needs more than this in worship.

Spontaneous worship in the classroom at moments of discovery and wonder will still occur with many older groups, but increasing self-consciousness may make this more difficult for teachers and pupils alike. If it becomes unnatural and embarrassing it is better left alone. Where it does arise naturally, however, it is to be valued.

The involvement of juniors in their own assemblies might emerge as a planned presentation of the life-themes the children are engaged upon. 'Light', for example, can be a theme for worship, the culmination of a class's work, sharing the paintings, writings, discoveries, and music about Light. In 'Jesus as the Light of the World', the analogy of light and its meaning can be explored through hymns and poems and prayers about light. Perhaps a 'Festival of Lights' could be planned. What could be a more fitting theme for Advent and a worship preparation for Christmas? Or even for Easter (the Light that could not be put out) or Whitsuntide (The Spreading of the Light). The language of worship should provide satisfying images. For the children, if it speaks in terms of images that are genuine products of their own experience or imagination, worship will answer their needs more effectively than an adult form of language speaking in terms of images which are unknown.

Topical events, important dates from the calendar, especially of the Christian year, and changes in the school are all valid worship themes if they are genuinely shared experiences. The welcoming of new staff and pupils or their leave-taking to other schools is often a rather perfunctory process instead of a joyous reception or sending out, in which the support of the whole school can be expressed and felt.

In the secondary school worship is often, quite rightly, more adult in form. It should not be as personal, in one sense, for it is important not to arouse deep-seated needs about which adolescents are very conscious, without offering some satisfaction of them. In another sense worship for the younger pre-adolescents, as well as the adolescent school population, should deal with real life experiences so that worship can be experienced as relevant to life. The fact that secondary schools, at present constituted, deal both with children and adolescents, is an argument for the division between primary and secondary education coming at twelve or thirteen years rather than eleven years. For this reason I have deferred a fuller discussion of worship in the secondary school to the next chapter.

GROWING FORWARD

Research in many subjects indicates that there is a change in intellectual quality among pupils generally in their thirteenth year. My own investigations indicate that this age also is a crucial age in religious development, for the potential of fuller conceptual thought about religion makes a maturer commitment to religion, or a rejection of it, possible in the ensuing years.

The beginning of adolescence brings with it emotional as well as physical changes. A perplexing situation, where religion is concerned, is that as our pupils begin to reach intellectual maturity and are able to deal with religious ideas more effectively, many of them at about the same time begin to develop negative attitudes to religion. The capacity to understand more is present, but motivation may deteriorate.

One reason for negative feelings about religion and religious teaching may be boredom. This is vividly expressed by a secondary school pupil, 'We used to keep going back over the same things and they'd flog the same old thing to death.'[25] Looking back over the suggestions we have made for religious education, I would hope, by trying to avoid 'too much, too often and too soon' in teaching the Bible, some of this boredom could be avoided. Given a content of religious education more in tune with the real needs of children, we can perhaps prepare a bridge into a religion satisfying to adolescents, rather than merely bring them to the edge of an unbridgeable chasm. Looking forward to the emotional and intellectual needs of adolescents we shall examine how well these bridges have been, or can be, constructed.

9

Adolescence

I AM USING the term 'adolescence' in a very general sense to mean the period, beginning with puberty, when the body of the child begins to grow into the body of an adult. Since there is a wide variation in the age when puberty occurs, I am choosing the approximate age of thirteen years quite arbitrarily as the beginning of adolescence for most of our pupils in secondary schools. Girls, we know, mature earlier than boys, but by the end of the thirteenth year, recent surveys reveal that most boys have begun to catch up on the earlier physical development of girls of the same age.

I am also limiting my discussion to the end of school age which for most is fifteen years of age but for an increasing minority continues until sixth form or its non-grammar school equivalent. It will be seen therefore that I am confining my generalisations to early and middle adolescence.

We have noted already the increased intellectual ability of most pupils, as they begin to think in more abstract or propositional terms (formal operational thinking). This does not appear to be related to the beginning of puberty in any significant way, but seems rather to be the result of widening experiences and the pressures to think more accurately and perceptively about them. So about this time in school there is a real 'break through' in most school subjects when childish modes of thought are left behind and a more adult intellectual quality is emerging.

The physical growth of the adolescent, however, does have several consequences for intellectual development, some of direct and others of indirect influence. The glandular changes in physical development, for example, lead to increased emotionality and a wider range of feeling. The emotional instability recognised as a feature of younger adolescents is an expression of this, before the young person has come to terms with himself. He needs to learn how to handle these increased and sometimes new emotions he is experiencing. Body changes also mean a self-consciousness very disconcerting for many adolescents, at a time when they wish to appear socially mature. The major experience in terms of physical maturing is, of course, in sexual development, the physical changes of the body being accompanied by a new awareness of members of the opposite sex. Socially, as a wider interest develops those relationships which had been of first importance begin to recede, and although there is still the need for the security and support that parents can give, it is a time when there is real conflict between their old ties in the home and those outside.

All this development leads to wider intellectual and social horizons, which stimulate and release a new questioning spirit which permeates all the interests of adolescents. As the Newsom Report states graphically:

> Boys and girls who used to ask enquiringly, 'What do we do?' or 'What's that?' now commonly react with 'Why should I?' or 'How do you know?' to much of what they have loved and practised in the past. They

become increasingly aware of the differences of opinion between adults and of the gulf between practice and profession. The borderline between cynical disengagement and constructive questioning is narrow (pp. 52-53).

This questioning is further stimulated by the commercial pressures of mass media, which strengthen the natural solidarity adolescents feel together and a narrowing conformity to 'the teenage image'. Some of this is superficial, but superficial or not, there is no doubt that a 'teenage culture' exists in the minds of our adolescents and exercises a powerful influence on values, behaviour and beliefs. In search of a moral authority as adolescents are, there is a real tension between the need to be sure and the need to be free. Peer values are now of great importance; the authority of adults must be supported by much more than mere authority.

The increased freedom and greater affluence within our society has spread to the adolescent section of our population. Young people are much more in evidence, they can be seen and heard much more than in times past, and the natural disapproval of older generations frequently breaks out into real hostility. So very easily adolescents themselves return this hostility and so 'the gap between the generations' widens. Parents, teachers and others who deal with adolescents can be readily identified as policeman figures of repression.

RELIGIOUS CHARACTERISTICS

About the age of thirteen marks a change in religious thinking as in other school subjects. Statements about religion and biblical stories can now be seen in less literal terms, as concrete modes of thought become less dominant. Propositions, ideas, relationships, can be thought of in more abstract terms, making the language of religion decidedly easier to comprehend. Most of our pupils at this age begin to conceive God in symbolic, abstract and spiritual terms. Some cruder anthropomorphic ideas of God linger on, especially with less able pupils, but in the main God is thought of as unseen and unseeable because he is a spirit. Divine communication is thought of, not by means of a human voice, but as mental, internal and subjective in the person concerned. Biblical literalism may still persist, yet there is a move towards a non-literal interpretation and a recognition of metaphorical, poetic truth. Alongside this is a much more developed sense of time so that historical sequence and some sense of historical continuity is possible, a very important conceptional development if religious history is to be at all meaningful.

I could illustrate in much more detail how this higher form of thinking about God, Jesus, evil, prayer, and the Church becomes possible in this period, but I have already described this fairly fully in the first volume. In brief we can say that there is a move away from childish thinking about religion and a desire to move forward to more adult concepts. Lest we see this in too optimistic terms let me add that this is more an intellectual potential than the real situation for many adolescents. This potential is realised more by brighter pupils, more by older pupils, more by girls and more by those in grammar schools. For many duller pupils, younger adolescents and boys this potential is not realised, and some in secondary modern schools do not achieve this higher level by the time they leave school.

The reasons for this can be explained partly in terms of changing attitudes to adults, partly because of an impatience with the content of much religious teaching and partly as a reflection of the age in which adolescents live. Negative attitudes to religion may well be closely tied up with growing criticisms of adults, and what more appropriate weapon is there to hand than religion, often associated in their minds with repressive ideas, adult authority and unquestioning obedience? Recent surveys indicate that adolescents feel the content of much religious teaching to be 'childish', revealing both their weariness of hearing the same stories and incidents already heard many times in their childhood, and their rejection of it as they search for a 'more adult' form of the truth. It may be that how adolescents are taught is as important to them as what they are taught, if they feel a new status is not given to them in recognition of the fact that they are no longer children.

Part of the discontent with the content of religious teaching is also the more advanced dualism which I discussed earlier. More systematic science teaching, a growing knowledge that not all teachers believe in religion, often open scepticism on the part of some teachers, all create a feeling that science and religion do not mix and that the supernatural and the natural cannot go together. They thus find much of the agnosticism of the age affecting their attitudes. Questioning which is ignored or clumsily handled leads to further expressions of doubt.

What stands out more than anything else is the desire of most adolescents to think for themselves. Since religion is ultimately a personal encounter with truth we should welcome rather than oppose such a desire. How this personalised thinking can be combined with helping adolescents to know objectively 'What do Christians believe?' is a matter we shall discuss later. Meanwhile we should note that adolescence is not so much a period of increased religious activity as a period of decision. By school-leaving age most young people have made up their minds to reject the Christian faith.

Many have taken a most positive decision and embraced it through confirmation or church membership. But churches report even here there is a substantial loss of young people immediately they have taken the step of joining a church. A fair proportion do continue within the church. My concern, frankly, is not so much about the numbers lost to the church, for no system of religious education within a secular educational system could produce a universal result, especially within the kind of society in which we rear our adolescents; my concern is that they should accept or reject Christianity on the right grounds.

By far the greatest proportion of our adolescent pupils who reject the Christian faith are those of lesser abilities. Many of them have not even achieved the level of full religious thought before negative attitudes have formed and a built-in rejection of belief has begun. These pupils have stopped thinking about religion long before they consciously reject it. The causes of this are a tangle of boredom, the association of religion with fairy tales, 'science has proved religion isn't true', its apparent remoteness from life and therefore an irrelevancy where real life is concerned, and a confusion with much of the language and thought used in the Bible. As the Newsom Report states:

Unfortunately, from a teaching point of view the syllabuses are less satisfactory, especially where the interests (and interest) of less able children [*sic*] are concerned. The general approach has been to start from Bible study—itself a difficult literary and historical art once the simple story-telling stage is over. From this source teachers are to build up by inference a general body of Christian teaching. This is to go a very long way round for most of the boys and girls with whom we are concerned and many of them get lost on the way (p. 57).

And yet a great deal of spiritual potential is there, often unexpressed or only vaguely voiced. This spiritual potential will be more evident as we look at the basic needs of adolescents.

BASIC NEEDS

What are the basic needs of adolescents which religion must satisfy if it is to make a valid claim upon their life and loyalty?

Security-in-Freedom

This period is a growing upward and outward, a crossing of the frontiers of new experience. It is marked by a desire to burst out of the restrictions of childhood. It is a necessary and desirable search for fulfilment, for the self can only grow in conditions of experiment and freedom. Fundamentally, all human beings having to meet new experiences and new pressures feel insecure until they have come to terms with them. This is why adolescence is so insecure a time of development. The stresses to be faced and the adjustments to be made are greater than at any period of human growth. Just as the adolescent needs freedom to experiment and to explore, he also needs secure bases from which to go out and to which he can return.

The merging of security-in-freedom is a delicate balance. If there is too great a freedom allowed, too much of it for the adolescent to handle, experiment can lead to disastrous consequences. If security is too protective, on the other hand, or too repressive, then adolescents will either fail to grow up as they should or they will endure it until they feel it to be intolerable and then break out recklessly. It is obvious that over the last four decades our society has become less protective of its adolescents as more and more freedom has been allowed them. We are still more protective of adolescent girls than of adolescent boys, but greater affluence and the availability of cheaper forms of transport have resulted in much greater physical freedom for both sexes in the last ten years.

In these years security is found within adolescent groups, which exercise considerable moral authority upon individual members. To be different, to voice too many deviating opinions, to dress differently and behave differently is agony for many adolescents, because if they do not conform, the rejection of their peers and the sanctions of the group will be visited upon them. Yet the real bases for security lie outside adolescent groups, even if the adolescents themselves have appeared to wholeheartedly abandon them for greater freedom. These bases are the home, school, community, church, wherever there are sympathetic adults whom adolescents love or respect, not because they can impose external authority upon them, but because they are seen as mature human beings who have stability and understanding. Security is in adults with whom trust has not been corroded by criticism, condemnation, repression, ridicule, jealousy or suspicion.

It is true that young people will provoke adults whom they trust, to see how far they can go, and so appear to invite negative or repressive reaction. But the gap between the generations can be bridged, rather than allowed to grow wider, by adults who accept this behaviour with understanding and good humour, as a natural expression of social experimentation. Adolescents are much more difficult to live with than are children. Perhaps this is why we allow children to experiment more freely than adolescents, whose needs are even greater.

Security then is rooted in persons, and secondary school teachers who are permissive, friendly, mature, themselves are contributing to this dual demand by adolescents and are answering one of their basic needs. The school community itself should reflect this attitude rather than that of a repressive institution. And if many of its members are Christians, the cumulative effect is to provide a spiritual setting in which the young can grow as persons in an atmosphere of trust.

Status

Basic to all adolescent experience is the hunger for significance and status. We all want to be accepted and respected, and for the adolescent his status is of great concern at a time when he is uncertain about his place in society. 'I am neither kid nor man, and get the worst of both worlds,' says one adolescent boy bitterly. It is a problem largely created by our society in that we do not provide greater responsibility for young people in any systematic manner as they grow older and more experienced. Many adults complain that young people do not want responsibility and will not behave responsibly when offered it. Invariably this is because they have not been introduced to it in an increasing amount. We must all be trained to be responsible people, coming to it slowly, learning how to take responsibility in gradually widening experiences.

Are we in secondary schools consciously planning for this? A prefect system, or responsibilities of this kind asked for in the final year of a school career, is a partial provision, and only caters for a small number within a school community. In secondary modern schools the course is so short for the majority that this is a pressing matter. Opportunity to discuss school matters, make suggestions about rules and decisions, help actively in the running of the school, participation in school councils, all indicate to the growing pupil that he is a member of a real community, not a cipher upon whom the community is imposed. Rules and standards are observed because they are 'ours' to ensure the smooth running of 'our school', and not imposed as irksome and meaningless directives by 'them'.

At a time when adolescence itself is a term of contempt, our pupils need to be assured of their worth as individuals. More far-reaching than all that we say is whether or not by our attitudes as teachers we show a respect for our pupils. Anything, by word or inference, which shows we regard them as children, boys and girls (how often these terms are used in assembly) or pupils, undermines their status and their belief that we respect them. Young person, young adult and student are more appropriate words to use. But more important is our underlying respect, our willingness to listen to their point of view, and to allow them to participate in what they are asked to do.

What has this to do with their religious education? A great deal, if trust and belief are not only rooted in ideas, but also in human relationships. Religious teachers pre-eminently must confer more and more status upon their pupils, encouraging an atmosphere of free exchange of ideas, to a greater and greater degree with their increasing age. When they reject much of their religious education as childish, it is not only the content, but it is because they think their teachers consider them to be children in presenting it by authoritarian methods!

This does not mean a disappearance of discipline, although discipline narrowly conceived only as a repressive administration of punishment is contrary to the respect adolescents need. Indeed, a religious teacher who cannot control his classes is a walking demonstration of the weakness and ineffectiveness of religion. Respect, friendliness and tolerance must be mixed with firmness, so that the school community can exist. Rules and standards, once decided upon, should be firmly enforced, but as the rules and standards of the whole community, not of the smaller numbers of teachers alone. But the rules in themselves are inadequate if there is no atmosphere of fellowship, sharing or respect for all members of the school. This lies essentially in the hands of the head and the teaching staff.

Idealism

Cynical detachment is the rather sad deterioration of an adolescent's natural idealism. So often there has been little attempt to harness the abundant energy or altruism of adolescents and what cannot be expressed dies all too soon. Of course, part of the teenage culture is to appear cynical and unconcerned, but beneath this mask there is a basic altruistic human need.

Sexual development means that a person is able to achieve a level of altruism unknown in childhood, simply because love as both a physical and emotional expression is a giving as much as a getting. With this comes a greater sensitivity to other people, especially to members of the opposite sex, and a new quality is seen in the adolescent's desire to be attractive and to please, not for authoritarian reasons, but because of heightened sensitivity to people. There is an accompanying growth of concern for justice, equality and freedom, rooted in what they want for themselves, but carrying implications far beyond adolescence. The tremendous support by adolescents for 'Freedom from Hunger' campaigns, Ban-the-Bomb movements and other causes are indicators of their need to identify themselves with idealistic movements and to be challenged by more than self-interest.

Does a secondary school community demand enough from this adolescent idealism? Schools ask a great deal from society in taxes, rates, personal help by experts, often voluntarily given. What does a school give to the larger community in return? Can religious education really be religious education without both challenging young people to serve the community and providing tangible opportunities by which this service can be expressed? If such challenges and opportunities are made it means that the teachers who make them must also give up the time and energy to organising service and themselves work alongside adolescents in a common cause. Such causes could be helping old people, hospital service, building a children's playground, raising money and collecting clothes for refugees.

Love

Adolescents, so often in love with love, are frequently regarded as objects of fun, and their first blundering attempts at relationships with the opposite sex, are dismissed as 'calf-love'. However comical or pathetic some of this must appear to adults, this is the area of his life where the adolescent stands in greatest need of help. His longing for love and to give love are also the emotional materials which make for religious insight and spiritual experience. Until we have loved, not at a childish but at a maturer altruistic level, can we really understand that God is love or know the appalling nature of the love of Christ upon the cross? It is in the elation of love, in the depression of love failures, in the feelings of love, rejection and guilty self-reproachments that perhaps the first effective intimations of the need for redemption are known.

A religious education which does not directly concern itself with this great dynamic of adolescence is inadequate and unrealistic, for the theme of love is the great theme of Christianity. When Harry (see page 19) at eighteen years of age says 'Religion is essentially love and yet very few religious people want to talk to us about sex,' he is perhaps forgetting that sex is only rightly looked at in the context of wider personal relationships. He is nevertheless voicing the needs of most adolescents who are seeking guidance. The Bible has a great deal of relevant teaching about love, but how arid and pointless some of it must seem beside the 'real' tumult of adolescent love. Obsession with sex, guilty habits of masturbation, and teenage fantasies of physical fulfilment reflect the pressures and values of our commercial society. Adolescents see the insincerities of a double morality in society but very easily succumb to what they despise. In this situation sex education in the school belongs more in the religious education periods than the biology lessons, for it is the clear distinction between love and lust, and the value of loving persons rather than bodies, which young people need to understand.

Meaning

Alongside the adolescent's search for an ideal and a love, there is his need to find a purpose. Part of this purpose is to fit all his experiences within a meaningful context, so that life makes sense. It may be that he will resort to a non-religious-pattern of a political or humanist tradition. Much more common is the retreat into 'cynical disengagement', because the search is too difficult and what he thinks religion has to offer does not make sense.

Our adolescents in the second half of the twentieth century are faced with a situation far more difficult than was apparent even thirty years ago. Applied science and technology now impinge upon their lives daily and the tempo of the age is that of affluence and materialism. More and more of our most talented young people are being trained for jobs involving scientific or technological techniques. Since the end of the last war we have belonged to post-atomic, space-exploration, synthetic fibre age, in which man's inventive ingenuity and material self-sufficiency is plainly demonstrated.

Does our religious education take the needs of a more thoroughly scientifically educated generation into account? It may be argued that the old controversies between science and religion are a thing of the past, settled by the scientists and theologians fifty years ago. This may be so (although I feel it is too optimistic an assumption), but these issues are still very much alive in our secondary schools. They may involve ill-informed notions of what both religion and science really are ('Science shows that the Garden of Eden couldn't be true, sir') and a great deal of time must be given to an exploration of the validity of differing ways of arriving at the truth. If in primary education there has been a consistent integration of knowledge, much of this two-world view may have been prevented. The chances are, however, that a science-theology gap will need bridging, as the most pressing intellectual problem to be faced if adolescents today are to find in Christianity an answer to their search for meaning.

THE CONTENT OF TEACHING

Intellectually at thirteen most adolescents are becoming capable of seeing the truths of the Christian faith, of understanding what Christians believe, if they are convinced by this time that it has something relevant to say to them. The problem of negative attitudes has to be faced, especially with less able pupils. This question mainly concerns the methods by which we teach religious education at this age, but it does also affect the content we should be teaching.

In the secondary modern school most of our pupils have two years more before they leave school. It would be tempting to spend most of this time trying to teach as many historic facts as possible, so they will not leave school 'ignorant' of the religious facts. But the question of motivation must be faced. If we start with religious or biblical themes they must in some way be linked dynamically with the real life experiences and needs of adolescents. Many grammar school pupils will be able to deal with the more objective and systematic examination of the facts, and it would seem appropriate to devise two different types of contents for the different abilities of pupils—a continuation of life-themes for the less able and 'religious' or bible-themes for the more able.

Although I shall discuss these two forms of content separately it would be foolish, as well as unrealistic, to see them as separate entities. There should be considerable overlap, and some teachers might do a few weeks of life-themes followed by another few weeks, or a term, of Bible materials. If two periods a week are taken for religious education, the two different approaches could be taken at the same time as parallel courses. Life-themes at this age should include a great deal of biblical content, and biblical-themes should obviously continue to link Bible experience with modern life.

Bible-themes

By the age of thirteen years our pupils should have covered briefly, not in great detail but enough to convey the general content, a simple life of Christ, largely to answer the questions, 'What did Christ do?' and, 'What did he teach?'. To lead them beyond the Gospels into church history it should be presented in a simple outline of the coming of Christianity to this country. Two questions should be explored. 'What effect did Jesus have on the world?' (A few illustrations from Acts and the Epistles, the Roman Empire and the spread of Christianity and 'Who is Jesus Christ?'). This last question prepares the way for a systematic looking back into the Old Testament, not a wearisome detailed study of history, but the growing awareness of the need for leaders and saviours in Hebrew history. To lead our scholars forward in their thinking by going back into the Old Testament is to invite comparison between the saviour figures of Israel and the kind of Messiah Jesus was. This explains the conflict, hostility and finally the condemnation of Jesus. He was to many of his day a false Messiah. Instead they expected another Moses, another David or a fiery Maccabeean leader.

In this way the Old Testament is not seen in isolation from the New, but the New Testament is being used as a yardstick to help our pupils exercise some critical judgments about the behaviour and beliefs implicit in the varied Old Testament religions. We are helping them to see the Old Testament through New Testament spectacles.

The saviour figures of the Old Testament will lead to a discussion of the situations from which the Hebrews needed saving, and the predicaments from which men have always needed salvation. Economic, military and moral situations can be seen within a Bible and life context, so that the Bible story can be understood in its total theme, with its great climax in the coming of a Messiah or Saviour concerned more with the inner spiritual condition of men.

As our pupils will by now have begun to enlarge their knowledge of history, especially British history, some parallels can be drawn between the history of Israel and that of our own nation and the key 'saviour' figures who command our respect. But these historical comparisons should not conceal the central and disturbingly personal nature of the question 'Who was Jesus Christ?' With the evidence before us of his claims and what the words show, we should stimulate our pupils to weigh these carefully. As a climax and also to present the issues dramatically a carefully prepared series of trials could be held with the class acting as judge, jury, advocate and witnesses, where the evidence is presented and examined.

The pattern of this type of Bible-theme is briefly:

1. *A Life of Christ*
   What Did Christ Teach?
   What Did Christ Do?

2. *What effect did Christ have on the World?*
   The Acts and the Epistles.
   The Spread of Christianity.
   Modern Society's Christian Roots.

3. *Who is Jesus Christ?*
   His claims compared with
   (i) Other Bible Saviours and (ii) More Modern Saviours.

4. *What do we need saving from?*

The movement chronologically is forward from the time of Christ to the present day, and only then a move back into the major personalities and events of the Old Testament. This will make more sense in that the Bible is seen as a continuity, and Old Testament narrative is not viewed in isolation but in a comparative context. What has the love of God in Jesus Christ to do with such deeds as the slaying of Goliath, the annihilation of whole populations of a city or the various condemnations of the prophets? The yardstick of Christian love is the measure which should be used to evaluate the partial truths of pre-Christians.

Lest this type of teaching is regarded as too abstract and too academic, let me suggest another type of Bible-theme which can be followed through systematically and chronologically. Some of these themes could be related directly to adolescent experiences, but all are linked directly to the major intellectual problems young people raise. I suggest that the major canvas of Bible teaching can be covered by helping our pupils to see the development of the following ideas:

What kind of God did they believe in?
How did they look at suffering?
The Bible looks at death.
What is right or wrong?
Different kinds of loving.

The list is almost endless when we see that would add the Bible's developing themes on Forgiveness, Salvation, Marriage, Slavery, Prayer, Law, Men, Fellowship with God, and many others.

This presupposes a view of the Bible as progressive revelation, not in the sense that there was always a clear-cut refining of ideas throughout the Bible (there are frequent regressions in thought and the picture is often confusing) but that these are the dominant problems men faced and slowly and painfully sought to answer them. Beginning with the spirit religion of the patriachs, we can trace their development through to the fullest revelation of God in the Incarnation.

This kind of intellectual journey, taking any major Biblical idea, is appropriate at this time because adolescents can look back at their own earlier primitive ideas of childhood, and so enrich their understanding of themselves. They can also see current reflections of old ideas in modern superstitions, the cult of astrology, belief in ghosts and the like. How many adolescents see the fascinating trail through the Old Testament into the New Testament of the Idea of God? It could be a whole course in comparative religions in itself leading from animism (patriarchal religion), the tribal god of war, a nature god of storm and violence (Mosaic religion), a territorial god of Canaan, an agricultural fertility god, (the Settlement), monolatry (Elijah). This leads to the move towards universalism and monotheism, the development of an ethical monotheism and divine judgment (the prophets), glimpses of the universal God of love (Isaiah), until the fuller revelation in the New Testament. Many adults have never clearly seen a progression of this kind; all too often they have become lost in the mass of detail, in which no discernable pattern has been visible.

Or again, to meet the needs of adolescents in a theme such as 'Different kinds of loving', the differences between philia, eros and agape can be seen in terms of the great love stories of the Bible. Take, for example, the story of Hosea.[26] A group of secondary modern girls were discussing the theme of love. A married couple, of religious conviction, came to the school, bringing their young baby with them, talked about what they felt love really is, and then answered frankly the girls' questions. This couple invited the girls to their house for tea.

In contrast to this happy home, the girls looked at the story of Hosea, of love in a broken home. One girl writes, 'There was a girl called Gomer, who was popular with the boys till she'd been out with them, and then they didn't like her any more. Hosea had fallen in love with her and his father and mother didn't like it.' The teacher got the class to imagine Hosea's mother writing to a women's magazine. One girl writes,

Dear Evelyn,
My son wants to get married to a girl who's got a terrible reputation. All the neighbours say she'll give him the push soon or go with other men when she's married to him and got fed up with him. What am I to do?

The answer is also imagined, 'Give this girl a chance to prove if she's suitable for your son.' The story of his marriage is explored, and told to the girls in their own terms, the coming of three children and of Gomer's desertion. The girls tried to express Hosea's feelings in love poems. Here is one of them:

I had a love, she loved me true
Then she left me for another,
And wherever she went my heart went to.
O Gomer I thought you were true!
The roses on the bushes are jealous
Of your sweet and tenderness
But like a rose you pricked my feelings
When away you went.

Other poems tell of Hosea's renewal of love when he meets her again, dirty, ragged and rejected by everyone. One girl imagines Hosea saying to himself, 'I wonder why I still love Gomer after she left me and gone with other men? Then he thought', continues the girl, anything we do wrong must hurt God, and he realised that God loves everybody, no matter what they've done.' The girls then begin to think of the ingredients of real love. 'You need patience,' says one, 'real love includes understanding, friendship, loyalty, unselfishness, getting on with each other's family, doing things together.'

I have written this account in some detail to illustrate how an imaginative teacher has used the experiences and insights of her girls to explore a Bible-theme. In these terms this is not instruction nor a presentation of facts, but a process of growing insights by stimulating them to place their own experience alongside the given experience of the Bible.

Life-themes

Some teachers may feel that both suggestions I make under Bible-themes are too academic for their pupils, no matter how frequently adolescent experiences are placed alongside the biblical material. They would argue that the disposition of less able pupils is against this type of approach and say that only by beginning with the concrete problems and specific questions of young people can real religious education take place.

Harold Loukes in *Teenage Religion* discusses a four-year course and suggests that the two different approaches be used. 'For the first three years, the Bible should provide the themes, historical, moral and spiritual, pressed as far as may be towards the contemporary historical, moral and spiritual situation. In the last, the present world, as immediately experienced by our young people, would provide the themes, which would be pressed back to the Bible where the same themes were originally, and so profoundly, explored.' My comment here is that while this may be a suitable balance for many pupils, it may still be too intellectual an approach for less able ones. We must be flexible about this and adjust the content to suit the pupils.

There is, of course, no reason' why the two approaches should not overlap considerably.

The Newsom Report (page 168) appeals for an information service on 'What Christians Believe' for adolescents.

> In their last years at school there is need also to help them see the difference that being a Christian makes, or should make, to the answers that have to be given to problems of living. Some of these problems are personal and immediate; some are collective and social—relations with parents and with friends of the opposite sex; problems of conflicting loyalties to friends and to moral standards; nuclear weapons and the colour bar; the care of the old and thalidomide babies.

Where possible, Newsom suggests that social studies and religious education should be closely associated.

Materials for life-themes on problems of this kind are available in the S.C.M. in Schools series.[27] They cover a wide range of adolescent questions; Getting on with People, Working for a Living, Talking about the Bible, Black and White, Fair Play, God and You, Taking your Choice, and Getting and Spending. Teachers often make their own materials or life-theme cards. A newspaper or magazine cutting may be used, with questions to be answered seriously. Two examples[28] are shown on pp. 185 and 186.

Printed materials of this kind can easily be made, but many life-themes can be introduced as the occasion arises in the normal questioning of young people. Teachers can, of course, be launched into answers to irrelevant questions by pupils only intent upon wasting time. But given the sincere and serious attempt to provide teaching of this kind, young people are not lacking in serious concern to make the most of the opportunity. In *Teenage Religion* (pages 117-44) Harold Loukes suggests ten basic life-themes and explores how they can form the basis of a syllabus suitable for middle adolescents. They are friendship, sex and marriage, snobbery, money, work, leisure, prayer, suffering, death and learning.

In an appendix Mr. Loukes sets out five lessons on the Christian View of Sex and Marriage. It is interesting that in a similar appendix to the Newsom Report a headmaster shows in some detail the policy of his school on sex education. The religious education department is a major partner in this school, together with health education, biology, housecraft and the teaching of other subjects. There is no shortage of this material in newspapers, magazines and programmes on television and radio. If these vital matters involving the closest personal relationships are not dealt with in some way within a religious context, alongside religious values, religious education can quite justifiably be dismissed by our adolescents as irrelevant.

The problem about life-themes, voiced by so many teachers, is its vagueness. There is no set pattern of lessons to be followed through, no ground to be covered. This problem is a very real one and the teacher who cannot overcome it would do better to confine himself to a Bible-theme syllabus. But given some planning ahead, an alertness to the needs of his pupils and an ability to exploit their questions, this type of approach has a great deal to offer.

World Religions

An inevitable part of adolescent questioning will be about other religions. In these days of immigration they

183

may be acquainted with Hindus, Sikhs, Buddhists and Muslims. In some areas of the country, I know schools where followers of religions other than Christianity have talked to the students about their faith. This is a lively and personal way of seeing the religion as a living faith, not a straw-religion with outmoded ideas to be easily dismissed. A good school library will contain many reference sources from which the young people themselves can gain objective information. It is fairly certain that many will want to look beyond Christianity before their final school year, but it is important that they should understand the essentials of the Christian faith before they begin to draw comparisons.

TEACHING METHODS

Much has been implied about how we should teach religion to adolescents in my discussion of the teaching content appropriate to their needs. While some information is required, and is often asked for, recent investigations have shown that what adolescents most resent in religious teaching is to be treated as information fodder. This resentment is not confined to the last year in school but is evident from about thirteen years onwards. In the natural rising tides of adolescent energy they want to question, to express doubts, to discuss and to explore ideas for themselves. This eagerness must be used, not repressed, so that a personal confrontation with religious truth can be made.

Whether we choose Bible or life-themes, it is plain that discussion methods must play a significant part in how we teach. Discussion may be between class and teacher, although because of the size of classes, this may

What will happen?

DURING the children's service I led prayers and asked the children to pray for the coloured people, explaining to them what was happening in South Africa and America.

After the service a small boy of eight said to me:—

"What will happen if all the white people who do not like the coloured people die and see God—and he happens to be black?"

V. I. Hughes.
96, Pattiswick Square,
Basildon, Essex.

1. Does it make any difference to a person if they are black ?

2. Why don't some white people like black people ?   3. Do you ?

4. Could God be black or white – and if not, why not ?

5. Did Jesus tell his disciples to go only to white people – and can black people be Christians ? (Look at Acts. Ch. 8 – remember that Ethiopians are black – and also at Matthew. Ch. 28. v. 19.

I know it's wrong—
but I want him to stay

"For two years I've been living with a married man," writes Carol. "I am 21. He is 31, has two children by his wife and two by previous girl friends. He said he would get a divorce and marry me one day but now he wants to go back to his wife.

"We've been so happy I can't face losing him. You may say he's unfaithful and that I should give him up, but there's so much good in him I know we could be happy again if only I could win him back."

CAROL must summon up all her courage and commonsense and let this man go. His weakness could almost be faced and overcome if he'd been unfaithful to one woman only, but he has obviously never felt a scrap of responsibility or loyalty towards anyone who's loved him and shared his life. The conclusion must be that he lives for himself alone and does not want to be faithful to Carol or, perhaps, to anyone.

He is, at last, doing the right thing in returning to his wife and children and I think Carol should charitably believe he's doing it for the right reasons. She mustn't try to keep him from this. She is still very young and has plenty of time to discover that there are men who do feel a loving responsibility for the women who love them and bear their children.

1. If the man hadn't had any children do you think he still needed to go back to his wife?

2. Could he really have loved Carol, and even if he did, was he right to live with her?

3. Could Carol ever be happy with him?

4. What do you think was the man's biggest mistake – and what should he do about it?

5. Do you think that what Paul says about love in 1 Corinthians 13 1-13 has anything to teach these people?

be the least satisfactory way in which it can be arranged. A more useful organisation of discussion is in small groups with class members as the leaders, so that all, even the least able, may participate. Discussion too should not be vague or too general but addressed to precise problems, clearly set out. A skilled teacher will see that the right facts are available to help discussion and a number of periods may have to be spent working individually or in small groups consulting books, collecting information or sorting various viewpoints, before an intelligent dialogue can take place. The teacher himself will be one source of information and some straight teaching can be used profitably, so long as it is set within the spirit of inquiry.

I am not suggesting that the teacher can or should be neutral. If he tries to be neutral the question will frequently arise, 'What do you think about this?' quite justifiably. But to answer this in the spirit of dogmatic assertion is bad education because it demonstrates a spirit contrary to the teacher's main intentions, to get pupils to think genuinely for themselves in their encounter with Christian belief. One of the basic needs of the adolescent we have noted is his need for status, the need to be valued and treated as a person. Teachers should be sensitive to this need, not only in the school community generally, but in attitudes conveyed in the classroom with individual pupils. The opinions of the least able should be listened to seriously, expressions of disagreement encouraged and not taken as personal criticisms, and thinking regarded as a co-operative effort, not a one-man band. If there is one bond between teacher and pupil desirable in all this, it is the bond of mutual trust.

The need for teachers to adapt themselves to a thoroughly different psychology is very urgent, for we know that from the third year onwards behaviour problems begin to increase as adolescents become more restless. Their resistance to dogmatism also increases as they develop the powers and the confidence to express their disapproval. These symptoms do not occur in schools where participation in learning increases with the age of the pupils, and where added status is given. For some teachers this may mean a reversal of how they see themselves. It may involve thinking as a member of a group rather than being the sole source of information, directing the work but also following it, answering questions but asking many more, learning as well as teaching, searching as much as finding.

By the use of methods of this kind, preparation is just as important as in the straight teaching lesson. Merely asking 'What shall we talk about today?' is to invite vagueness. The teacher must know clearly what areas he wants to cover and then seek by every possible means to engage the interest and participation of his pupils. But the best plan for content, organisation of the class, work to be done, material to be consulted, should yield flexibly to the changing situation. No set pattern or structure of a lesson is possible but, as Loukes suggests, three elements should be present in all considerations of a problem. There should firstly be an attempt to clarify the problem, to identify and understand it. Then what Christians believe in relation to it should be explored. And finally what would happen if that teaching were genuinely accepted and applied should be faced.

The best teaching in religious education I have ever seen has been with teachers who have used these personal methods, both in secondary modern and in grammar schools. For in these kinds of situations there has been a meeting of minds, a stimulation on both sides to think, a hammering out of personal belief and disbelief in genuine partnership. Many grammar school pupils can look forward to the freedom of the higher forms where personal discussion is the normal pattern of teaching. But we need also to try to achieve something similar to a sixth form experience for secondary modern school leavers during which their minds, however limited, may openly explore the profound problems which face them. This experience may never again be theirs once they have left school.

WORSHIP AND ADOLESCENTS

Secondary school assemblies are a very mixed bag, some enjoyed by the pupils and others hated and criticised. My object here is not to report the present situation but to suggest the forms which most closely meet adolescent needs.

First of all, the sense of occasion of the meeting of the whole school is valued by pupils. Many, even the most sceptical, having left school often report it to be the feature of school life they most miss, as though when they begin work they 'haven't started the day right'. This may merely stem from the loss of a well-worn habit rather than any real religious deprivation. It is probable that what they miss is the sense of a community coming together. Perhaps this is felt more strongly because there is no other experience comparable to this, for the majority will long ago have ceased to attend church services. For many this is their only

'Church' experience and they stand in need of a community which will sustain and support them. Poor halls, overcrowded conditions and having to stand for assembly create problems, but even working within these conditions real worship can and does take place in secondary education.

The general level of worship should be aimed at adolescent needs, despite the presence of many in the first two years who are technically pre-adolescent children. Even these will look upon themselves in 'the teenage image', as they enter secondary education and will regard themselves as having left their childhood behind. The tone of worship will therefore be more adult, although this will not mean that only adults lead or participate in it.

Worship, as with any other age groups, must be related to real life and, while it should have dignity, must be couched in language genuinely expressive of adolescent needs. It is valuable, therefore, if the religious education department of a school can plan assemblies, so that they are related, not always too closely, to the themes of classroom teaching. The role of head of the school is an important one but the leading of assembly should certainly not be his monopoly. Themes of a class investigation may reach their climax in school assembly, being the presentation and showing by a class of what they have achieved. Sometimes a problem, posed in the setting of worship, may be heard in a five minute playlet put over 'live' or recorded on a tape.

Whether or not classroom themes be expressed in worship, there should be a clearly organised topic running through any one morning worship. I come across schools where the Bible reading is chosen by the religious education specialist, it is read by a pupil chosen by the head, the hymn is chosen by the music specialist and the prayer by the person conducting the assembly. Training for audible reading or announcing is presumably the province of the English department! This extreme case is an absurd situation, for the persons responsible for the assembly, members of staff or pupils alike, should try to plan it as a unity. Perhaps members of one department will plan the worship. If, for example, it is the English department it may be more in the nature of a poetry reading, if the music department then music may provide the major theme, but why not history, science, housecraft, metalwork departments? The more varied the participants the more assembly will be an offering of the whole school life to God.

The more formal structure of hymns, prayers and readings will be a frequent pattern. Petitions for the school, individual members in danger or in need, prayers of forgiveness, of aspiration, of praise—the whole variety of Christian prayer can now be used.

There is nothing really new I have to write about adolescent worship. What is most striking about assemblies meaningful to this age group is the sense of community and the lifting of the heart in praise. Sometimes the sheer beauty of a piece of music, a poem, a prayers, will come home. These moments may be rare but are worth planning and hoping for. The contribution of worship to religious education is incalculable and intangible, for if we can succeed for a few moments in bringing the school face to face with the mysterious transcendant power behind all creation, we shall have achieved far more than all our education about religion.

GROWING FORWARD INTO ADULTS

Since we have confined ourselves to the contribution of the school to religious development we must take our leave as teachers of them long before they have achieved full maturity. Even with the best religious education we can devise many of them, even a majority, will not reach the point where they can embrace Christian beliefs either as they leave school or later as adults.

With some there will be an act of faith, supported by an intelligent appreciation of why they believe and what it can mean for them. But with the others, is it worth all our time and effort, and the frequent disappointments experienced in the communication of religious truth? It will have been worth while if they grow on into adult life more perceptive, more sensitive and more aware of what life holds for them. They should know, however partially, what it is they cannot accept or have rejected, not because it is confusing, childish or absurd, but because they have not found it true to their experience, or because having known what it implies they see it asks too much. At least they will understand something of the debt our society owes to the Christian faith, and not least they will have savoured a human relationship of trust and care, with permissive and sympathetic adults, in whom this belief is a reality and a power.

10

A Total View

THE TIME HAS COME to move away from the specific details of the last few chapters and to take a total view of what I have suggested as a suitable pattern consistent with the development of children and adolescents today. This pattern is what I would call 'Developmental Religious Education'. I would like to make it clear that this pattern is put forward as a series of positive suggestions based upon much more research data than my own. To make this book more readable I have tried to cut footnotes down to a minimum, but those familiar with recent publications will notice that I have merged a great deal of my own thinking with that of Acland, Daines, Hamilton, Hyde, Loukes, Wright and of the team who produced the University of Sheffield Institute of Education report.[29]

The authors quoted, and whose findings I have used, are in no way responsible for the interpretations I have made, nor are they committed to supporting my conclusions. Yet the cumulative evidence all appears strangely to converge upon several important points for religious education. First, the complexity of religious concepts as compared with the limited intellectual development of the young. Second, poor attainments in terms of Bible knowledge after many years of Bible teaching in schools. Third, an increasing sense of the unreality and irrelevance of religious teaching as childhood is left behind and adolescents begin to think for themselves. Fourth, the importance of motivation and attitudes in the formation of religious ideas and beliefs. Fifth, the incremental nature of religious growth and learning, depending upon many varied experiences of life. And finally, there is a unanimous conclusion that the current syllabuses for religious education in our schools and the methods by which they are generally taught are quite unsuitable in the present situation.

Much of the research and writings mentioned diagnosed the situation and our problems, but there are many positive implications on which there is a great deal of agreement. These may be summarised in the following terms. Religion and life are one and if religion is to be apprehended and believed we must constantly keep religion and life together, not separate them. Religious truth must be seen by children and adolescents to be true in their own experience in a twentieth-century setting. The young, even from their earliest years, should be encouraged to participate in their own religious education so that their insights and their conclusions are the result of a personal encounter. The Bible is not a book for the young, but it may, when placed alongside life in a relevant context, challenge, clarify and strengthen personal convictions in them. Equally, if used too soon and irrelevantly, it may retard religious thinking and create negative attitudes and be a disservice to religious teaching. The quality of human relationship is the major formative religious influence in childhood and adolescence, and all that is taught stands or falls by the kind of relationship which exists between teachers and their pupils.

Although these assertions are widely supported not only by research, but recognised in practice by many experienced teachers, the implications about what we shall do in religious education in our schools are not easy to see. When we descend from the generalisations into particular recommendations many criticisms will arise. I must confess quite frankly that it would have been easier for me to have remained in the general sphere of research writing, but I have felt compelled to go further and make more specific and concrete suggestions. I am aware that what I have written is vulnerable, but I have advanced it as one contribution towards the present re-thinking taking place in religious education. My justification for doing this is that whereas most researches have been applied to one area of school life, my own investigations have spread over the whole span of compulsory schooling.

The total view put forward in this book may be seen in terms of content in the visual chart on p. 196. I wish to stress I advance this picture in no dogmatic spirit. If it is accepted as a sensible and workable progression it must still be regarded experimentally and applied with a great deal of flexibility. In all visual presentations there is a necessary over-simplifying and I have only put in ages in the chart very reluctantly. It is obvious that some children of a given age range will be ready for the suggested approach, but for others it may not be appropriate. The ages stated, therefore, are only meant to be rough guides.

The shape of the chart is not intended to have any educational significance (does the narrowing shape of the diagram symbolise the narrowing of teaching under the influence of the eleven plus?). Where the

PRE-RELIGIOUS THOUGHT

SUB RELIGIOUS THOUGHT

PERSONAL

RELIGIOUS

THOUGHT

Infant school (Early Childhood) 5-7 years.

Early Junior School (Middle Childhood) 7-9 years.

Late Junior School (Late Childhood) 9-11 years.

Early Secondary School (Pre-adolescence) 11-13 years.

Late Secondary School (Adolescents) 13 years plus.

School-Leavers (Adolescents)

Enriching General Experience and Artistic Expression. Spontaneous worship in classroom and use of Children's Spontaneous Questions. Themes based upon these.

Continuation of General Enrichment by Across-subject teaching. Begin elementary Life-themes, some leading to Festivals.

Religious themes: Simple Life of Jesus. Bible background facts. 'What is the Bible?'

More advanced Life-themes in across-subject projects and activities.

Religious Themes; 'What is the Bible?' More advanced Life of Jesus. Some Acts.

Some Life-themes for less able pupils.

Life-themes and problem-centred exploration for less academic pupils.

Religious Themes: A Bible chronology—
N.T. forward into Spread of Christianity to modern Britain; Back into O.T. 'Where it began'.
Or Bible themes—developing ideas from primitive religion O.T. to N.T.

Sex education in terms of relationships and personal values.

Adolescent problem-centred discussion 'What do Christians Believe?' Some comparison of world religions.

A Visual Model of a Programme of Developmental Religious Education throughout Schools band appropriate to a stage of development is divided into two parts, this is to signify that either suggestion may be taken or the two combined in alternate or consecutive teaching. Readers who want to explore the suggestions in more detail should return to the appropriate chapters, but I have deliberately not enlarged upon what I have written so that teachers can explore and develop the suggested themes for themselves. We have provided 'The Readiness for Religion' Series for children as examples of possible materials for use in primary and early secondary schools.

What I have tried to do in this scheme of developmental religious education is to present a child mainly with those ideas and truths which are within his experience. Beginning with a very generalised experience and working forward into more specific ideas, I would lead children to integrate all they are learning and doing in all subjects within a world view of God as creator and as the person who cares about his people. Religious, biblical or other related experiences, are fed in sparingly at first, not in increasing quantity but in increasing complexity, so it is a higher quality of thought which is required with increasing years and experience. The language of religion then becomes not a mere religious vocabulary, but the language of the child's experience, and a consistent picture is being built up of religion as relevant and real. Even though some of the material comes from long ago and far away it is all of a piece with present-day happenings. In this way the two worlds of religion and science are held firmly together. Where in the final year of the junior school or early in secondary school critical thinking about the Bible is encouraged, within a belief that it is 'a true to experience' book, some of the problems of adolescent criticisms are anticipated in a constructive manner. A great number of limiting crudities, concrete limitations and literal misunderstandings will persist, but these will not be reinforced by our teaching, and bridges are being thrown forward into the next stage of thought.

The situation necessarily changes with the move into secondary schools where the class teacher gives way to the subject teacher. More 'straight' religious teaching now becomes possible, but it is better to slowly work at the assumptions we make about the Bible, about truth and proof, about belief, even as we begin a more systematic biblical study. Even so, less able pupils in the beginning of secondary schooling will need a diet more nearly resembling primary school themes than that of their more academic peers. After the first year or two there is a period when most of our pupils could cope with a short but substantial examination of the Bible. I suggest two possible ways of accomplishing this, both of which feed in factual material for later exploration of 'What Do Christians Believe?' The really skilled teacher will integrate a great number of life situations and adolescent problems with this approach, but many times these may have to be treated separately. It may be that this should be the major emphasis when dealing with more backward pupils.

Where the Bible is concerned it is important not to attempt a detailed coverage. There is so much detail that our pupils may not see the wood for the trees, or more appropriately, the Word within the words. It is enough that in a few typical samples they see the quality, the grandeur and the wonder of what the Bible is saying to them.

Alongside this, I am suggesting that the most pressing problem which already the adolescent is facing, that
of sex, be seen as part of the religious education syllabus, and treated within the wider problem of human
relationships and personal values. Again the skilful
teacher may use a Bible theme to illustrate the personal
values which are the basis of human relationships, as an
introduction to the problem, or leading from the problem to wider related questions. In the final year we return almost full circle to the personal quest of experience we began with in the infant school. What Loukes
calls adolescent problem-centred methods should be
used, alongside the major question 'What do Christians
Believe?'

I am aware that there are many criticisms which can
be made, and educational questions arise at once about
syllabuses, teachers and examinations as well as those of
a more theological nature. I will now try to face some of
these criticisms and attempt to provide some answers to
them.

THE IMPEDIMENT OF PRESENT SYLLABUSES

Many local authorities are considering a revision of
their syllabuses of religious education. We have had
some revisions in the past but they have mainly repro-
duced the same Bible-centred type of courses, which are
the subject of much criticism. Even very recent revisions such as that of Bristol (1960) not only continue
with many of the old ideas, but perpetrate quite a few
new inappropriate ideas for young children. There are
one or two notable exceptions, such as the Carlisle,

Cumberland and Westmorland (1951), which have made brave experiments with various types of courses. On the whole, however, few changes have come because revisions were begun, and often completed, before the present findings of research were available. The first authority to take these findings really seriously is the West Riding syllabus, revision of which is eagerly awaited.

Meanwhile, it will take a long time before these newer ideas spread and agreed syllabuses throughout the country develop a new pattern. It may be several years before changes appear, to help teachers towards a more suitable content for religious education. Are the present syllabuses an impediment to the type of content suggested in this book, and must teachers wait for the syllabuses to change before trying to implement these new suggestions?

There are three reasons why we should not and need not wait for wholesale syllabus changes. The first is that the present syllabuses say little about how religious education should be taught. Many by implication or silence appear to suggest that oral, straight teaching, mainly by story-telling, and the imparting of biblical knowledge, is the only acceptable method. But activity and project methods, personal investigation and discussion, full participation in the ways I have proposed, are in no sense in conflict with present syllabuses. The revolution required in religious education is in the methods of teaching as much as the content. Much of this depends not upon a series of educational gimmicks, but upon the quality of personal relationships, how far we are willing to trust our pupils, and other factors not within the control of any syllabus. In his most recent investigation Harold Loukes[30] notes that in many schools 'the "knowledge" and intellectual concepts with which "religious instruction" deals are not being satisfactorily dealt with, but the personal relations established in the process are conveying something of value.' 'Personal caring is more significant than teaching', reports Loukes.

The second reason why present syllabuses need not impede immediate changes by teachers is to be seen in the realm of worship. Syllabuses make some suggestions about worship but the suggestions are meant only to stimulate. There is nothing at all to prevent a much more exciting and experimental approach to worship through our pupils' real life experiences, and by the artistic offerings and sharing of the pupils themselves at every stage in the school system. There is a great deal of unrealised potential in school assemblies as a power in the religious education of the whole school. Many schools do experiment. Other schools keep to a fairly predictable pattern and achieve a high level of sincere reverence. But all too often worship is not related enough to what is being done in the classroom, and vice versa. Changes here need not depend upon syllabus changes.

Finally, we must face the fact that if we take the introductions to agreed syllabuses seriously, we must recognise that teachers have the right to select, prune and modify very drastically the content suggested by the syllabuses. Many authorities not only tell teachers to 'avoid following the syllabuses slavishly' but urge them to interpret the content very flexibly in the light of the differing needs of their pupils, when they translate the syllabuses into their own schemes of work. The

Cambridgeshire note 'On the Use of the Syllabus' is fairly typical.

> The compilers wish to make plain that the object of the syllabus is to serve as a guide and not as a hard and fast scheme of actual lessons ... for the use of the teacher, who, it is hoped, will study the syllabus as a whole, and, in using any section of it, *freely adapt the material or add to it in accordance with his own ideas and the needs of his pupils* (my italics).

Let me be very forthright about this. If a syllabus, compiled before research revealed problems of religious thinking, recommends, shall we say, an historical account of the Exodus and occupation of Palestine, which is plainly inappropriate for early juniors, the teacher of these children has every right to eliminate this section 'in accordance with his own ideas and the needs of his pupils'. If life-themes are taken for juniors, *some* of the biblical material recommended may be appropriate, and the teacher is then, in the context of children's needs and experiences, 'freely adapting the material'. This indeed is what is already happening on a large scale, where teachers are plainly dissatisfied with the syllabus, and have a serious concern for their children. Such teachers are neither dishonest nor ingenuous. They are in the best tradition of British education in using the syllabus as it is meant to be used.

All the life-themes I have suggested, and all the material made available in the 'Readiness for Religion' series can be used within the total scheme of any agreed syllabus, in that much teaching of the material recommended will occur in teaching 'from the Bible' in the context of relevant life-experiences. More New Testament material will be used than Old Testament material, and probably a greater variety of biblical material generally will be encountered by the pupils. The problem of the syllabus is greatest in primary schools, and it is here where teachers need the most encouragement to adapt freely.

HOW SHOULD SYLLABUSES BE REFORMED?

Nevertheless, a radical reform of agreed syllabuses would give a positive support to teachers and remove many of their doubts and difficulties, if the needs and capacities of children and adolescents form a central concern in the planning of the content. I use the word reform advisedly, since a revision in most cases would appear to be inadequate. Syllabuses need to be reformulated on a very different basis, and a start from a fresh beginning would seem more desirable than trying to amend the existing structure. A glance at the type of biblical material mentioned in the chart on page 196 will show why. Although free adaptation is recommended by syllabuses, many teachers do follow it slavishly.

There are two ways in which reform is urgently needed. The most obvious is in terms of the type of material recommended and the way in which the Bible itself is regarded. Agreed syllabuses tend to be based upon the assumption that the Bible is the textbook of religious education and, as such, should be adequately covered during the years of schooling. The Bible may be a book for adults to study, but it is demonstrably not a children's book. Adolescents are just beginning to be capable of moving about within its pages freely. The major reform required is a new orientation so that the needs of twentieth century children are the starting point, and that educational insights now applied to other subjects can be seen as relevant to the teaching of religion. I would crystallise this in the following terms:

(i)   The needs of pupils—emotional and intellectual—should be our first concern. A term such as 'chil-centred religious education' can be misunderstood, but if used in the correct sense indicates the starting point.

(ii)   The limitations of children's language, experience and intellect should be accepted realistically, so that the level of complexity of thought demanded by religious thinking shall be the major consideration when grading content suitable for differing ages.

(iii)   Religious education in a general sense begins with the young, but is mainly a period of preparation for Christian education, which only becomes possible (in a theological and intellectual sense) during secondary schooling.

(iv)   A clear distinction should be made between 'teaching the Bible' (seeing it as a religious textbook) and 'teaching from the Bible' (seeing it as true to experience rather than a monolithic body of truth).

(v)   The content of a syllabus should prepare children to think rigorously in religious terms, to be imaginative in their response to religion, and to explore its truths for themselves.

(vi)   In adolescence, objective and factual information about Christianity is important, but this should not replace the spirit of enquiry and the personal search young people ask for.

(vii)   To obviate a mass of material 'to be got through' themes should be suggested in very brief outline, on the principle that they should be added to rather than selected from.

(viii) Where scriptural reference is noted, the life experience it is meant to illuminate should be set out parallel to it.

e.g. 23rd Psalm { The Care of Parents.
{ Experience of Shepherds.

Hosea   Adolescent love problems.

This would act not only as a guide to teachers, but would force a syllabus committee to keep its feet on the ground of real life.

I could continue developing a number of points here, but it would be advisable to address myself to the question of how I envisage the 'content' recommendations in this book could be set out in syllabus form. I do not anticipate any committee accepting the plan of content I set out as a syllabus. All I have been concerned to do is to produce a tangible alternative to the present situation, based upon what I interpret as being the implications of research to date. In some ways my plan suggests schemes of work, more than a syllabus, but a general pattern is clearly discernible which could form the basis of a syllabus. There is a great deal of detail to be worked out within the themes, both life and religious themes, suggested. Some of the detail should be worked out by syllabus committees, but a great deal should undoubtedly be left to the teacher. Any child-centred plan will inevitably entail this, to make it flexible enough to allow for adaptation to the needs of children.

It will be seen in the diagram on page 196 that no provision is made for alternative courses until half-way through the junior school. This is because the generalised and informal work with infants, and the life-themes for young juniors, provide a great variety of material and activities covering a very wide range of ability and interest. Illiterate or near illiterate children can find out and do many things, while there is enough to stimulate the brightest child. This is still true of the themes suggested for older juniors, but some less able children will find the concepts demanded by the Bible theme 'What is the Bible?' too difficult. For this reason a syllabus using this as a basis in these years should provide workable alternatives for less able children. The 'What is the Bible?' theme would be more appropriate for these pupils in early secondary schooling.

I would recommend, therefore, serious planning in syllabuses for less able pupils from nine years onward, with alternatives more experientially based. At the other end of the ability scale, grammar school streams probably need no special provision since the same content (of religious themes from 11 years onwards) can be used at a higher level by a teacher of such pupils. It is easier to have a 'normal' secondary modern based syllabus to be adjusted upwards, than to have a grammar school based syllabus, too academic in the first place, which has to be adjusted downwards. The norm in a secondary school syllabus should probably be 'B' stream, with separate suggestions for 'C', 'D' streams and below.

The second way in which reform of agreed syllabuses is needed is in the setting out of material and a clearer choice suggested. For example, as we have noted, current syllabuses, sometimes by default, imply no choice of material and also that the method shall be one of instruction and story-telling. Guidance about how a syllabus may be used should not be confined to the introduction, where it may be overlooked, or once read, forgotten. Recommended material, themes, activities should be so set out that even the most unperceptive teacher will be able to see that there is a choice, that a choice once taken may be elaborated upon, and that there is no need to 'race through the syllabus' or 'cover the ground'. Quality of insight achieved, rather than quantity of content 'done', should be the constant emphasis. Without going on at great length, syllabuses should continually indicate alternative methods to story-telling and presenting factual material. Anything which encourages the teacher to implement things to be done by the child is to be commended.

Local education authorities have responsibilities beyond producing a reformed syllabus. Once the syllabus is printed, copies should not merely be sent to every school, and the matter left there. Nor is an official launching of the syllabus enough. A well-organised attempt should be made to interest all teachers who will use it, both primary and secondary, by introducing, explaining, and illustrating how it may be used, to small groups of teachers. Better still, many schools may have been invited to 'try out' suggested material and write in critical comments, before a syllabus reaches its final form. Even so, after it is completed a period of about twelve months of helping teachers with a new syllabus is needed. At primary school level it could be based on a school staff or a joint meeting of two or three school staffs in an area. At the secondary school level, the specialist religious teachers will make suitable groups. Too often a syllabus may be stillborn because no further impetus is felt to be necessary than printing and distributing it.

I am also not at all sure about the wisdom of printing

it in book form. This is not only a very expensive process but it has a finality about it which may prevent further emendations and changes which may arise as a result of trial and experience. Syllabuses in other subjects are constantly revised as new insights and new techniques become available. Have our agreed syllabuses been most resistant to this process because of the form in which they are presented? Small spring folio binders allowing portions to be added, discarded or replaced would seem to be more sensible. The speed with which society and the influences upon children are changing seems to suggest that a full scale review of an agreed syllabus should not be less than every ten years.

OUTSIDE INFLUENCES INTERFERING WITH CAREFULLY SELECTED CONTENT

Many teachers have raised this question with me at conferences, and it is a very important one. Suppose the content is carefully arranged in a developmental progression, based upon the readiness concept, there will be many outside influences which will interfere with our carefully planned ideas. Fundamentalist Sunday school teachers or clergy, the even more fundamentalist Bible-epics on the cinema screen, the scores of children's books, broadcasts, television programmes and other influences which emphasise the separateness of religion would appear to endanger their religious thinking and reinforce childish concepts. An example of this is a well produced, beautifully illustrated, children's educational weekly, otherwise excellent, but in its religious material extremely literal. A copy on my desk as I write presents Moses, with an account of the Exodus which is literal in the extreme. It shows a dramatic picture of Moses waving 'his rod and the waters of the Red Sea separate to allow the Israelites through'. Among other information the children are told, 'Moses died aged 120'. This article is flanked on one side by an accurate account, with illustration, of the process of the distillation of petroleum, and on the other by a similar scientific presentation of the life of the beaver. No clearer reinforcement of a two-world view could have been designed.

This kind of interference, of course, is happening in all subjects and is not a problem confined to religious teaching. Well-meaning, over-anxious parents will get children to 'do sums' before their number concepts have developed, and will get them to write and read prematurely. Many bad habits in many skills are formed in this way and have to be broken down before other effective learning can take place. Yet this kind of 'interference' has not intimidated teachers of other subjects from persisting with carefully planned sequences of teaching.

Outside influences are usually haphazard and sporadic. The teacher's influence within a consistent frame of reference will be much greater, especially if he is willing to use these outside experiences when they are referred to by the children, instead of ignoring them. Was Cecil B. de Mille's version of the Exodus in *The Ten Commandments* following the straight biblical narrative the only one? If you had been a film producer, how would you have presented it? In such a context ideas of the Bible as myth, legend and interpreted history can be discussed. The conflicting authority of a parent or clergyman is a somewhat different matter.

But we should be honest with children when this contradiction is expressed in class and 'other points of view' presented. Many teachers waver at the thought of this conflict. By avoiding it and being less than completely honest we are allowing these outside influences to undermine our whole educational aim. Yet the consistent frame of reference, which we bring to bear upon all our religious teaching, does help the child to resist or to re-learn effectively.

EXAMINATIONS

In secondary schools I have been asked, how can your suggested programme be reconciled to the examination system? There are, of course, two examination systems, referred to here. One is the internal system of termly or yearly tests for assessment purposes within a secondary school. The other is external examinations, such as the G.C.E. or the new Certificate of Secondary Education.

The unfortunate influence of some examinations is sometimes to narrow the teaching of a subject so that the examination paper tends in effect to become the syllabus. Where religious education is concerned it has another unfortunate effect of reinforcing teaching *about* religion and reducing much of the learning to memorised knowledge. Internal examinations need not have this effect if the examinations or tests are designed to make pupils think about some of the ideas they have covered during the course of the term or the year. Imaginative teachers of religion can, and do, prepare provocative questions demanding imaginative insight rather than regurgitation of memorised fact. Rather than 'Describe the events of the Crucifixion' why not

'You were a blind man until three years ago when Jesus of Nazareth healed you. Today you saw him crucified. Describe how you felt.' One question asks for facts, the other compels an entry into an experience.

Where external examinations are concerned it must be remembered that the C.S.E. was specifically intended to be in the control of teachers, although the first indications are that many teachers seem to prefer a central examining board. But if teachers will use their powers open to them, the examinations in religious education could be similar to internal school tests, with a mixture of insight and fact as the basis of the questions. Some regions have designed examinations based upon such titles as 'Christian Citizenship', where knowledge, insight and sometimes practical work is part of the assessment. But where only a diluted factual form of G.C.E. papers become the norm, teachers and individual schools should have the courage to abandon the C.S.E. in religious subjects as inappropriate to our major aims in religious education.

Both levels of the G.C.E. examinations are of undoubted value for brighter adolescents, who have had a sustained course of religious education based upon life-themes, and have been introduced to some critical religious ideas. As a preparation for intending teachers or those going into higher education generally it could be beneficial, provided teachers provoke a great deal of critical thinking. In a grammar school, preparation for G.C.E. religious papers should not mean the exclusion of such pupils from the religious discussion session normal in the fifth and sixth. Since examination candidates in this subject may sometimes have a pietistic or narrow frame of reference it is all the more important that they should be exposed to the vigorous questioning and doubts of their peers.

WE HAVEN'T THE TEACHERS FOR
THIS KIND OF APPROACH

It is true that developmental religious education is more demanding and asks for skills and imaginative ideas many teachers are unused to displaying in their teaching. Are we asking too much of teachers, for qualities many of them do not possess? I would like to apply this question to primary and secondary school teachers separately.

Where primary school teachers are concerned across-subject teaching is quite a familiar pattern. Infant teachers are usually flexible enough in many subjects to let subjects and ideas arise naturally. In junior schools, projects and activities are common enough for most teachers. It is true that many are still subject minded and unwilling to practice more progressive and less formal methods. That is why we have devised the 'Readiness for Religion' series, to help teachers, through the provision of children's materials, to recognise the possibilities and exciting potential in this approach. On the whole it is primary school teachers who are most critical of present agreed syllabuses, for they see that their assumptions and methods are out of step with other subjects they are teaching. Teachers also, who have been bored themselves with the perennial round of scripture stories, often show a renewed interest in the enormous variety of work possible in life-themes. Because they may become more interested and better motivated towards the subject, there is the chance they will become better teachers. Certainly, many of those involved in the training of primary school teachers are anxious to train new generations of students to this approach.

Secondary school teachers may find this kind of religious teaching more difficult. I am thinking not only of the specialist teacher, who may or may not have had some theological training, but also of the proportion of teachers in any secondary school who 'help out' by taking it as a second or third subject. Certainly, for these teachers it is less demanding to have set portions of the Bible to get through. The head of department, if a department of religious education exists in a secondary school, should be more than a co-ordinator of work, but the one who inspires and informs his less qualified or experienced colleagues of the best ways to teach. The majority of suggestions I have advanced for adolescents have stemmed from listening to specialist teachers talk about their work and the many experiments they have tried. With these teachers too there is a growing criticism of current syllabuses as too academic and too remote from life. A small but vocal fundamentalist section of teachers will find both the methods and content of my approach quite unpalatable. There is still a great need for far more supplementary training courses for religious teachers, with the emphasis not entirely on theology and bible study but with the religious development of the young and modern teaching techniques also included. Despite this, however, I am convinced the vast majority will find the thematic approach for the secondary schools both acceptable and practicable.

A few teachers have raised this question with some anxiety, and some restraint for this reason is to be seen in the Newsom Report, when it suggests that religious education and social studies be closely associated. The problem is simply that where religious teaching takes place in set periods on the timetable the legal requirements for withdrawing children, whose parents do not wish them to participate, can be easily observed. Where across-subject teaching on life-themes may cut across the timetable and specifically 'religious' material is part of it, can the law be carried out? What happens to such children in a class project for juniors, for example, on 'Light'?

I trust my answer does not sound obvious or evasive, but it seems to me that this presents no real problem. In all projects, life-themes and other topics, there are many alternate activities suggested for the children. Some of the activities may be 'religious' and others may be secular! Since most of the activities and teaching will be done with small groups rather than whole classes, children to be 'withdrawn' from religious education will be working with groups involved in the 'secular' material. For example, on the first work-book on 'The Source of Light' pages 5, 6, 7 and 13 could be left undone by a 'withdrawn' child. He would concentrate upon the physical discovery of light and enrich the class's knowledge by being able to do this kind of work at greater depth. Where a whole lesson is devoted to a 'religious' aspect of the theme, the matter is simply dealt with as before and children go to another room or carry on with another activity.

The problem is not entirely unknown in other subjects. Are such children withdrawn in an English poetry lesson where an anthology with some 'religious' points is used in class teaching? Are they withdrawn in history or geography when religious characteristics of a people are examined? Are they withdrawn when 'religious' music is played or sung in a choral music lesson? Is a teacher debarred from expressing her wonder in religious terms when the beauty of nature is appreciated, and are 'religious' themes in art classes vetoed because one child is 'withdrawn'? It seems to me we should keep a sense of proportion about this, while respecting the law and ensuring that the rights of parents are observed.

There is one interpretation of the law in another direction, which causes difficulties for some primary school head teachers. Their experience tells them that assemblies are sometimes better for their children at times of the day other than the beginning. The 1944 Act states that each school day shall 'begin' with an act of worship. The intention of the legislators was surely not to emphasise the time at which this happens, so much as to ensure that the assembly should be held daily. If assembly is held at any time appropriate to the needs of the children and the better running of a school, I submit that the law is being adequately observed. Perhaps inspectors and advisers could reassure experimentally minded headteachers in this matter.

NO SYSTEMATIC COVERAGE LEADING
TO NO TANGIBLE RESULTS

Many teachers are troubled by the apparently haphazard and vague content of life-themes, which they feel do not cover anything systematically. Many are also concerned that any results of teaching in this way may be rather intangible. The two criticisms are, of course, closely related. It is true that where any unfamiliar territory is to be explored, the landscape may have few recognisable features. Because it is unfamiliar we lack the assurance we normally display in familiar surroundings. The content suggested, however, is not entirely unfamiliar, since in illustrating experience *from* the Bible we shall be using quite a lot of familiar material.

Yet the problem of systematic coverage remains. The flexibility and choice of themes suggested for primary schools, which is one of the major advantages, do create problems for the teacher, especially one used to thinking of religious education as covering the Bible in a sequence of historical events and stories. The method may appeal but the content is felt to be 'vague'. This, of course, is a common criticism of most projects, because where more than one subject is involved the coverage is less substantial in every detail.

Within a given theme there is no reason why the material should not be covered systematically. We know what we want and we can plan for it as any sensible teacher does in planning a series of lessons. A series of experiences are explored in systematic order and related together in a religious theme. The order is not necessarily historical, chronological or biblical, but there is an order provided by the teacher and by the child's relating all that is learned together. Where 'Light' is explored, for example, all the aspects of Light—scientific, poetic, artistic, inspirational and religious—are very thoroughly explored in an ordered sequence. There is no vagueness in the planning, in the materials provided, nor in the ground to be covered. Pupils will emerge from it much more sensitive to the significance of light, both in terms of its physical properties and its religious meaning, than if conventional junior science lessons on light and a religious lesson on 'Jesus, the Light of the World' had continued in separate periods of the timetable largely unrelated.

The problem is greater when we look at a total school career, for the question is asked in relation to how systematically religious ideas, and especially biblical ideas, are to be covered. Does the end result at the completion of this kind of religious education add up to any orderly acquired total knowledge? I am tempted to quote the findings of the Sheffield study to indicate the very meagre end result of an apparently systematic coverage (of the Bible) attempted in the agreed syllabuses used in that area. The major defect was that the orderly progression and systematic coverage were present in the minds of the teachers, but not in the experience of their children.

Let me take the junior school as an example of what coverage should normally occur. In the first two years the following life-themes may have been explored: Homes, Birthdays and Parties, Shepherds and their sheep, Bread, the Seasons, Fire. These will have been linked, as a starting point or climax, with a specific Christian festival. Homes, Birthdays and Parties, The Seasons with Christmas; Shepherds and their sheep, The Seasons with Easter; Fire with Whitsuntide, Bread, Shepherds and their sheep, the Seasons with Harvest.

In the later period of junior school perhaps the

following life-themes will have been explored: Myself, Creation, Light, and Names, together with a first life of Jesus and an introduction to 'What is the Bible?' Again, there will have been direct links with festivals and a great deal of varied biblical material will have been used.

In the secondary school the more familiar coverage of Bible ideas is apparent from the third year, but the order is only chronological where it coincides with the ability of pupils to see order and system in it. Even here it is the chronology of how ideas developed as much as what events occurred, which gives pattern and coherence to the content. The final year of a problem-centred method may again appear to be formless and unsystematic, but the order is readily perceived, and sometimes asked for in more specific terms by the pupils themselves. 'Tell us what other religions teach', 'What is the Christian belief about Marriage?' or 'Is God black or white?' should be looked at systematically, not in short oversimplified answers.

It will be essential in junior schools to keep a careful record of themes treated by a given class, which should be passed on to each new teacher of the class from year to year. For the occasional child the repetition of a theme could be endured (although a new facet of the theme could be explored if already worked on). For whole groups to face repetition could be fatal. A simple class-cumulative-record would be simple enough to keep and to pass on and so avoid this problem.

The total result will be far from intangible. If what is meant by tangible is memorised fact, we could hardly do worse than the results of the present situation. There is a good chance that we shall do very much better, even in terms of knowledge. For knowledge is best retained when it is learned in a meaningful context, and one object of the Bible-themes recommended for later secondary school pupils is to provide this precise framework of meaning. In addition to all this, if at the end of our course religion is found to be a stimulating intellectual challenge, if it is seen to be relevant to real life, and if its essential offer and personal challenge is apprehended, these are 'real' results as tangible as any educator would desire. I do not claim that these results will inevitably happen. All I suggest is that there is a chance, with a programme of developmental religious education, that they may happen.

IS IT REALLY CHRISTIAN EDUCATION?

There is a genuine concern that the kind of programme I have suggested as suitable for the primary school, at least until the last year where 'religious' material is recognisably present in a systematic manner, is not only educationally vague, but is also theologically suspect. It has probably been noticeable to the discerning reader that throughout this book I have used the term 'religious' education very frequently, and 'Christian' education much less frequently. This has been a deliberate policy on my part, for reasons I shall examine shortly. I would first of all like to look at this very pertinent question, 'Is it Christian education?' in general educational terms and then in a more theological manner.

An educational parallel is the university professor of mathematics looking at play materials for number activities in an infant school and saying, 'The children really seem to enjoy this and it seems to suit their needs, but is it mathematics?' In similar terms we can legitimately enquire whether measuring the playground is geography? and whether some of the national legends and myths we tell juniors are really history? Such contents are not mathematics, geography or history in a fully-formed adult sense. Sorting of beads may seem so remote from the Honours Mathematics course as to have no connection at all with the final goal. In fact number is mathematics in the sense that it is the first partial step to an understanding of the world of counting and measuring, estimating and calculating.

Now this parallel is an appropriate one if we similarly dismiss pre-Christian and preparatory religious education as not Christian. It is not Christian in any finalised sense in that all the profound doctrines of the Christian faith are being taught. It is Christian in a preparatory sense, in that we are preparing children for the time when they can understand the Christian faith adequately enough to commit themselves to it or reject it as unbelievable. Can we call a premature attempt to teach Christian truths, which retard, impede and even prevent a person believing, Christian education? Is catechetical teaching, learning Christian doctrine parrot fashion, Christian education? It *is* in intention, and apparently in content, in that the 'right' theological language is being used and specifically Christian ideas are being taught. If, however, they are not being communicated, it is not Christian education. Mere conditioning is not education.

This is the reason for my usage of 'religious education' since it means we are trying to make children spiritually sensitive to the religious nature of their lives in a general sense, as preparation for their later encounter, in terms of their own experience, with the Christian faith. A beginning must be made somewhere and because Christian education cannot emerge fully formed, in an intellectual sense, in early childhood, this is no reason to dismiss the earlier preparatory stages as unworthy, trivial or not meriting the concern of Christians.

There are, however, good theological grounds for answering this question positively. From the earliest years in school I have suggested that all learning be held within the context of the belief, spoken and unspoken, that 'this is God's world and all that we learn is learning about the divine creation'. This could be dismissed as a mere pantheistic device, if it were not for the fact that the doctrine of God, the Creator, is one of the doctrines of Christianity. It is a specific starting point which provides a doctrinal basis to our religious purpose. It is not vague pantheism but is rooted in a God-centred view of life. The fact that worship is addressed to God, who possesses the quality of love and concern for his children, surrounds this assumption with a clear Christian conviction.

Where juniors are concerned this same atmosphere, and the assumptions which issue from it, continues. But the idea of across-subject projects based upon life-themes, in which religion and life are integrated rather than separated, has sound theological merit. There is the work of Tillich, stressing the importance of God's immanence, as well as his transcendence, as the groundwork of all our being. There is a real sense in which, because of their egocentric nature, the concept of God's immanence in their own experience is more natural to

children than ideas of his transcendence. To begin even
to apprehend this truth is the beginning of Christian
teaching, and in a sense I have been trying to apply
Tillich to the classroom situation.

But is this Tillich only? If we go back to the world's
greatest teacher we see that this is the way in which
Jesus taught. The Gospel record shows that he sometimes taught from the Old Testament scriptures, but
the major emphasis is his teaching from life. What we
often fail to see is that the stories we now try to communicate as Bible authority began as life-centred experience to illuminate or cast doubts upon traditional
ideas and attitudes. Perhaps we should end our book
upon this note.

JESUS—A LIFE-THEME TEACHER

Think of the real-life experiences of which Christ's
teachings speak, from which many stories emerge, and
many sayings originated. Sabbath day, ears of corn,
rest, sharing a father's inheritance, coins, playing in the
market place, sick people, foxes, wild birds, sparrows,
figs, taxes, boys on a farm, girls at a wedding, mustard
seeds, yeast, bread, builders, fishing, moneylenders,
thieves, wolves, money hoarding, bandits, kings and
slaves, rude guests, parties, beggars ... and so the list
could go on. When we recollect that this teaching was
with adults, we then realise how an appeal to experience
was central to his teaching. He did not talk about religion. He talked about life, but compelled people to see
it in a new and demanding context.

This life theme teaching can be seen not only in the
content but in his methods of teaching also. Professor

A Total View

Paul Torrance has written of this profoundly. 'In a way, it is strange that Christian educators have insisted upon teaching largely by authority, since Jesus himself was such a good example of the creative learner and the creative thinker. The first picture we have of Jesus after his birth and infancy shows him asking questions—one of the basic techniques for learning creatively.' He suggests that this inquiring tendency stayed with him all his life and that the Scriptures record 154 questions asked by Jesus. Torrance continues:

> As a teacher, Jesus also aroused the curiosity of others. People asked him many questions. He always treated their questions with respect and helped them find the answers. Of course, he may have answered their questions by asking them several of his own, to make them think. Jesus recognised thoroughly and acted upon the old law of teaching, 'Excite and direct the self-activities of the learner, and tell him nothing he can learn for himself.' Instead of giving ready-made solution Jesus threw people back on their own resources. Habitually, he would throw in a question now and then that broke up the serenity of his pupils and made them sit up and think.[31]

It is salutary to ask in this context, was Jesus himself a Christian educator?

NOTES

Notes

PART I

[1] For example Diana Dewar: *Backward Christian Soldiers*, London, Hutchinson, 1964.

[2] A summary of this research and the implications can be seen in my first volume, *Religious Thinking from Childhood to Adolescence*, London, Routledge and Kegan Paul, 1964, in Chapters 1, 2 and 15.

[3] See Chapter 4, *Religious Thinking from Childhood to Adolescence*.

[4] William James: *The Varieties of Religious Experience*, London, Longman, Green 1902, p. 31.

[5] I am indebted to Miss C. M. Parker for this illustration in 'Thinking Aloud about Religious Education', *National Froebel Bulletin*, No. 149, August 1964.

[6] For a visual chart of how a religious concept developed see *Religious Thinking from Childhood to Adolescence*, p. 17.

[7] See John Bowlby: *Child Care and the Growth of Love*, Harmondsworth, Penguin Books.

[8] Michael Argyle: *Religious Behaviour*, London, Routledge and Kegan Paul, 1958.

[9] I am indebted to Dr. F. H. Hilliard for making this distinction so clearly in the symposium on 'Readiness for Religion'. in *Learning for Living*, May, 1963.

[10] C. M. Parker: 'Thinking Aloud about Religious Education', *National Froebel Bulletin*, No. 149, August 1964.

PART II

[11] I am grateful to Miss M. E. Franklin, Headteacher of Keep Hatch Infant School, Wokingham, and the Director of Education of the Berkshire Education Committee for permission to quote from children's spontaneous comments on page 80 and from a tape-recorded discussion of teachers on pages 95-96.

Notes

[12] See Chapter 7 in *Studies in Education: First Years in School*, London, Evans Bros., 1963.

[13] See *An Infant Teacher's Religious Education Diary*, by Philip and Frieda Cliff, for further suggestions. This is in the 'Readiness for Religion' series, London, Rupert Hart-Davis, 1965.

[14] Sybil Marshall: *An Experiment in Education*, Cambridge University Press, 1963. pp. 157-9.

[15] Ronald Dingwall: *Shepherds and Sheep*, and Margaret Hughes: *The Importance of Bread*, London, Rupert Hart-Davis, 1965.

[16] I am grateful to Mr. J. Pugsley, Headteacher of the Sandy Lane County Junior School, Bracknell, and to the Director of Education for the Berkshire Education Committee for permission to quote from pupils' prayers and hymns.

[17] I am indebted to Mr. C. C. Reeve, Headteacher of Brinton County Primary School, Norfolk, and the Chief Education Officer of the Norfolk Education Committee.

[18] Heinz Kuhne: *Creation*, London, MacMillan.

[19] Constance Parker: *About Myself*, London, Rupert Hart-Davis, 1965.

[20] William and Inga Bulman: *Light*, London, Rupert Hart-Davis, 1965.

[21] Norman J. Bull: *Symbols*, London, Rupert Hart-Davis, 1965.

[22] Eric Rolls, Eric Lord, Constance Parker and William and Inga Bulman: *What is the Bible?*, London, Rupert Hart-Davis, 1965.

[23] Alan T. Dale: *How the Good News Began* (Mark's Gospel) and *The Good News* (from the Gospels of Luke and Matthew), in the New World Series, Oxford University Press, 1966.

[24] By kind permission of Mr. A. M. K. Simpson of the Victoria Park County Secondary School, Manchester, and the Chief Education Officer of the Manchester Education Committee.

[25] Harold Loukes: *Teenage Religion*, London, S.C.M Press, 1961.

[26] I am grateful to Mrs. Hester Oliver for permission to quote from a talk given in the B.B.C. Home Service on June 4th, 1964.

[27] *Thinking Things Through*. London, S.C.M. Press.

[28] I am indebted to Mr. B. D. Earl of the County Secondary Modern School, Wooton Bassett, and to the Chief Education Officer for the Wiltshire County Education Committee for permission to reproduce work cards.

[29] A list of the publications to which readers may wish to refer is:
R. Acland: *We Teach Them Wrong*, London, Gollancz, 1963.
J. W. Daines: *An Enquiry into the Methods and Effects of Religious Education in Sixth Forms*, University of Nottingham, 1962.

Notes

R. J. Goldman: *Religious Thinking from Childhood to Adolescence*, London, Routledge and Kegan Paul, 1964.

H. A. Hamilton: *The Religious Needs of Children in Care*, London, National Children's Home, 1963.

K. Hyde: 'Religious Concepts and Religious Attitudes' in *Educational Review*, February and June 1963.

H. Loukes: *Teenage Religion*, London, S.C.M. Press, 1961.

D. S. Wright: 'A Study of Religious Belief in Sixth Form Boys' in *Research and Studies*, October 1962.

University of Sheffield Institute of Education: *Religious Education in Secondary Schools*, London, Nelson, 1961.

[30] I am indebted to Harold Loukes for permission to quote from 'New Dimensions in Christian Education', S.C.M. Press, London, 1965.

[31] E. P. Torrance: 'Religious Education and Creative Thinking' in *Education and the Creative Potential*, Minneapolis, University of Minnesota Press, 1963, pp. 89-99.

INDEX

Index

Index

Index

Index